# Target
## Get back on track

**GRADE 9**

AQA GCSE (9-1)
# English Language
# Writing

Robert O'Brien

**P** Pearson

# Contents

# ① Generating ideas – narrative and descriptive writing

This unit will help you learn how to generate ideas for a narrative or descriptive writing task. The skills you will build are to:

• identify your intention

• create original, engaging ideas

• give your creative writing a satisfying ending.

In Paper 1 of the exam, you will be asked to tackle a creative writing task such as the one below. The question will give you a choice of two options: one descriptive, based on a picture stimulus; the other narrative, based on a straightforward story prompt. This unit will prepare you to plan your own response to this question.

**Exam-style question**

You are going to enter a creative writing competition.

Your entry will be judged by a panel of people of your own age.

**Either**: Write a description suggested by this picture.

**Or**: Write a story about a time when you felt threatened.

(40 marks)

The three key questions in the **skills boosts** will help you to generate ideas for narrative and descriptive writing tasks.

① How do I identify my intention?    ② How do I create original, engaging ideas?    ③ How do I give my creative writing a satisfying ending?

Look at one student's story plan on page 2. It was written in response to one of the tasks above.

**Exam-style question**

Write a story about a time when you felt threatened.

| | |
|---|---|
| 1. I arrive at the meeting point some way from city. | Set in the future, windy streets, include some futuristic details. |
| 2. I listen to the leader's speech. | Feeling inspired – unity with the other rebels. |
| 3. I leave with heartened comrades. | We feel ready to defend what is ours. |
| 4. There is an unexpected attack by government forces. | Confusion and violence. |
| 5. I flee in desperation. | Description of city in distance – contrast. |

**①** Write down ✎ **three** ways in which the writer of this story is trying to engage and entertain the reader.

.............................................................................................................................................

.............................................................................................................................................

.............................................................................................................................................

.............................................................................................................................................

.............................................................................................................................................

.............................................................................................................................................

.............................................................................................................................................

.............................................................................................................................................

**②** Can you think of any ways in which you could make this story even more interesting or exciting? Note ✎ your suggestions below.

.............................................................................................................................................

.............................................................................................................................................

.............................................................................................................................................

.............................................................................................................................................

.............................................................................................................................................

.............................................................................................................................................

.............................................................................................................................................

.............................................................................................................................................

# ① How do I identify my intention?

The first stage in planning any piece of creative writing is to decide on your overall aim. You need to bring characters and events to life in a well-organised and compelling way but you have a host of options at your disposal when determining exactly how you will do this.

**?** What kind of story is this going to be?

**?** Who is telling the story?

**?** How do I want my reader to think or feel?

Below are examples of some aims you might want to achieve in your creative writing alongside some methods you could use to achieve those intentions. You can, of course, combine two or three to create a more complex, multi-layered description or narrative.

**Aim**

| 1 Engage and thrill the reader. |
| 2 Create tension to keep the reader in suspense. |
| 3 Illustrate a moral message for the reader to take away. |
| 4 Unsettle or intrigue the reader. |
| 5 Draw the reader in to a static or dynamic scene or situation. |
| 6 Make the reader think seriously about an issue. |

**Method**

| A Use graphic analogy to real-life topics; invite empathy with characters/circumstances. |
| B Describe fast-paced action; use first-person narrative to create sense of immediacy. |
| C Build atmosphere of mystery or menace; withhold key details until the end. |
| D Have a character undergo a conversion or learn a lesson from events. |
| E Use unexpected or changing viewpoints; introduce twist in plot. |
| F Use evocative and atmospheric description to depict setting/events. |

① Draw a line 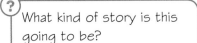 to link each method to the aim it would most likely help to achieve.

Now look at a developed version of the narrative idea sketched out on page 2. The plan has been remodelled from a different point of view to create tension and to make the reader think about an issue.

| From my hideout, I can see rebels listening to leader's speech and cheering. | I know it will all be over as soon as they turn round and discover me. | At the last minute, an unexpected attack by government forces disarms the rebels. | I am rescued and the rebels are captured and punished for their insubordination. |

② Choose one of the aims above and revise 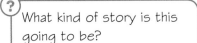 the plan to produce a different effect on the reader.

You could add intrigue by adding a second narrative voice, or increase the suspense with a last-minute twist.

# 2 How do I create original, creative ideas?

You will need to portray an original idea for your creative writing. For the descriptive task you can either use what you can see, or imagine what you cannot see, and then describe it engagingly.

(1) Re-read the descriptive writing task on page 1, then refer to the aims and methods listed on page 3. What is the main intention of a descriptive writing response? 🖊

...........................................................................................................................

With this intention in mind, here are two ways of approaching the descriptive task:

- **Fictional**: without telling the story as such, describe a setting for an imaginary narrative
- **Non-fictional**: describe it as a scene that you might have witnessed in real life.

Non-fictional description might seem the less complex option, but the advantage of the fictional approach is that you can create a more intense atmosphere, lifting it out of the ordinary.

(2) Look at the photo of the beach. Choose either the fictional or the non-fictional approach. Note down 🖊 any interesting ideas and evocative phrases that the image suggests to you.

| Interesting ideas (e.g. about situation, human activity, wildlife, mood, etc.) | |
|---|---|
| Evocative phrases | |

Choosing one of the following techniques will help you to structure your ideas:

- **Chronological** – describe an event over time from when it started, possibly using flashback
- **'Camera angles'** – capture a moment in time as if a camera were moving around the scene; zooming in and out; panning or tracking; 'seeing' different things.

(3) Plan 🖊 your chronological description in four sections using the table below.

| Dawn | 9am | Midday | Dusk (or flashback?) |
|---|---|---|---|
| | | | |

(4) Now 🖊 fill out the table in a similar way for a 'camera angles' structure.

| 1. (e.g. aerial view...) | 2. | 3. (e.g. zoom in...) | 4. (e.g. panoramic view) |
|---|---|---|---|
| | | | |

**How do I give my creative writing a satisfying ending?**

The ending of your story is likely to remain fresh in the mind of your reader and therefore needs careful planning. Try to ensure that it is given the space and weight it deserves and satisfies the expectations raised by the beginning and middle of your narrative.

**Exam-style question**

Write a story about a time when you felt threatened.

There are several ways you can round off your writing in a satisfying way. Look at these three different techniques one student experimented with.

**A** You can suggest that things are moving in a certain direction, leaving the reader to imagine a new phase in the story, e.g.

> *All around them lay destruction and chaos. But in an odd way this only stiffened the surviving rebels' resolve. Far from despair, they felt an unwarranted sense of hope that this was not the end, but in fact a new beginning. One battle was over, but another was yet to start.*

**B** You can focus on the closing thoughts and feelings of the main character, e.g.

> *Above the treetops, the skyscrapers of the great city could just be made out. Casper thought, 'Perhaps the leaders can see what has been going on here – surely they will come and help,' but he swiftly suppressed the idea, realising that, if this were the case, he would probably not be standing in the clearing, looking up to the sky in despair, mourning the death of a dream, the glimmer of hope, the light of a candle in the boundless darkness.*

**C** You can resort to a lucky new development or a change in direction (but this works best if it develops out of the narrative – otherwise, it can feel too unlikely or forced), e.g.

> *A dead branch on the ground cracked near where Casper had just been standing. He froze, then glanced furtively over his shoulder, not wanting to give away his presence. An injured rebel fighter was crawling towards him. Casper ran to help him up. 'Come on,' the fighter said through clenched teeth. 'It's up to us now. We've got work to do.'*

(1) (a) Which of these three types of ending do you think is the most effective? Tick it. ✓

(b) Write ✎ a sentence or two explaining your choice.

.........................................................................................................................................

.........................................................................................................................................

(2) (a) Look at the plan you wrote opposite in response to the descriptive writing task on page 1. On paper, write three possible endings to your story idea, using the above approaches.

(b) Which technique do you think works best in the context of your story? Why? ✎

.........................................................................................................................................

.........................................................................................................................................

# Sample response

To respond effectively to a creative writing task, you need to:
- choose an angle on the task that appeals to you personally
- be willing to risk expressing quirky and original ideas
- organise your ideas into a clear structure
- use plenty of atmospheric description
- aim at sharp, consistent characterisation
- depict engaging thoughts and feelings
- invent realistic dialogue
- leave enough time to come up with a satisfying ending.

Now look at this exam-style writing task, which you saw at the start of the unit.

**Exam-style question**

Write a story about a time when you felt threatened.

Look at one student's plan for this narrative writing task.

**1** How would you develop the plan? Add 🖉 some ideas of your own.

- I, a robot, 'wake up' (although it's not clear I'm a robot at first).

- 'Princess' (a scientist) comes over as my rusty joints stop clanking.

- Description of lab and Princess, while I 'gear up'.

- Threatened by a man (another scientist) who wants to destroy me.

- Manage to see off the enemy in some way.

# Your turn!

You are now going to **plan** your responses to both the exam-style tasks from page 1 and then write 🖉 your response on paper.

1. Note 🖉 all the ideas you might use in your plan for the **descriptive writing** task.

.................................................
.................................................
.................................................
.................................................
.................................................
.................................................
.................................................
.................................................
.................................................
.................................................

2. How will you structure your descriptive response? Tick one. ✓

☐ Describe an event over time

☐ Capture a moment in time

3. Who will your characters/narrator be? 🖉

.................................................
.................................................
.................................................
.................................................

4. Write down 🖉 some interesting descriptive phrases you might use.

.................................................
.................................................
.................................................
.................................................
.................................................
.................................................
.................................................
.................................................

1. Note 🖉 two different story ideas you might use in response to the **narrative writing** task. Sum up each idea in just one sentence.

Story idea 1:

.................................................
.................................................
.................................................
.................................................

Story idea 2:

.................................................
.................................................
.................................................
.................................................

2. Which of your ideas could, when developed, make the most interesting and entertaining story? Why? 🖉

.................................................
.................................................
.................................................
.................................................

3. What is the intended effect of your story on the reader? 🖉

.................................................
.................................................
.................................................
.................................................

4. What genre will you write in to serve this intention? 🖉

.................................................
.................................................
.................................................

# Review your skills

## Check up

Review your response to the exam-style question on page 7. Tick ✓ the column to show how well you think you have done each of the following.

|  | Not quite ✓ | Nearly there ✓ | Got it! ✓ |
|---|---|---|---|
| identified my intention | ☐ | ☐ | ☐ |
| created original, engaging ideas | ☐ | ☐ | ☐ |
| given my creative writing a satisfying ending | ☐ | ☐ | ☐ |

Look back over all of your work in this unit.

Note down ✎ the two most important things to remember when planning a narrative writing task.

1. ........................................................................................................

2. ........................................................................................................

Note down ✎ the two most important things to remember when planning a descriptive writing task.

1. ........................................................................................................

2. ........................................................................................................

## Need more practice?

Tackle one or both of the tasks in the exam-style question below.

### Exam-style question

You are going to enter a creative writing competition.

Your entry will be judged by people older than you.

**Either**: Write a description suggested by this picture:

**Or**: Write a story about a time when you experienced a shock.

(40 marks)

How confident do you feel about each of these **skills?** Colour ✎ in the bars.

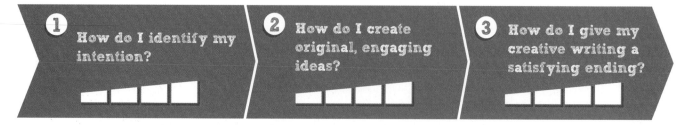

① How do I identify my intention?

② How do I create original, engaging ideas?

③ How do I give my creative writing a satisfying ending?

# ② Generating ideas – writing to present a viewpoint

This unit will help you learn how to generate ideas when you are writing to present a viewpoint. The skills you will build are to:

- identify your intention

- develop your ideas

- plan an effective conclusion.

In Paper 2 of the exam, you will be asked to tackle writing tasks such as the one below. This unit will prepare you to write your own response to this question.

---

**Exam-style question**

'We all need famous role models – they inspire us to pursue a purposeful life.'

Write an article for a national broadsheet newspaper expressing your views on this topic.

(40 marks)

---

The three key questions in the **skills boosts** will help you generate ideas when you are writing to present a viewpoint.

| ① How do I identify my intention? | ② How do I develop my ideas? | ③ How do I plan an effective conclusion? |

Look at one student's plan on page 10.

Most people's idea of a famous person is contained in the word 'celebrity', and we are encouraged to admire them.

But we don't all need celebrities – some find role models in family and people they know.

For those who do 'need' celebrities, they don't necessarily have a good influence – can have the opposite effect.

Examples of celebrities who can lead young people astray; attention-grabbing opposed to real talent.

Some famous people, though, do have a beneficial impact.

The value of famous people from the past (though they are not usually regarded as celebrities).

It would often be better to find our heroes in the past – we can be more certain of their overall value.

Moral choices and identity.

In the end, this is what matters.

1. What point of view is emerging from the above plan? Tick ✓ one statement below that you think best fits.

? Famous people are not reliable role models – people should be more self-reliant.

? Many famous people are wonderful role models, but the modern celebrity often is not.

? Famous people are essential as role models – we need them to inspire us.

2. Are there any points you would prefer to remove from the plan? Note down ✐ which ones, and explain why; alternatively, say why not.

.................................................................................................................................

.................................................................................................................................

.................................................................................................................................

.................................................................................................................................

3. Think of two ideas of your own to add to this discussion. Make a note ✐ of them below.

.................................................................................................................................

.................................................................................................................................

4. One idea in the plan above has no development in the right-hand column. Write down ✐ two or three ways you might build on that point.

.................................................................................................................................

.................................................................................................................................

.................................................................................................................................

# 1  How do I identify my intention?

Before you can generate ideas for your writing, you need to decide on your point of view – what opinion you intend your response to convey. One way to develop your point of view is by thinking about the possible points of view of others. Then you can focus your attention on how best to convey your own.

> **Exam-style question**
>
> 'We all need famous role models – they inspire us to pursue a purposeful life.'
>
> Write an article for a national broadsheet newspaper expressing your views on this topic.
>
> (40 marks)

(1) Add ✎ four or five ideas about this topic to the spidergram below.

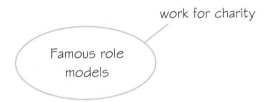

(2) Now think about possible views on the topic, bearing in mind that your audience is the readership of a national broadsheet newspaper. Put a tick ✓ or a cross ✗ next to each thought bubble, according to whether you want to include this point of view in your response or not.

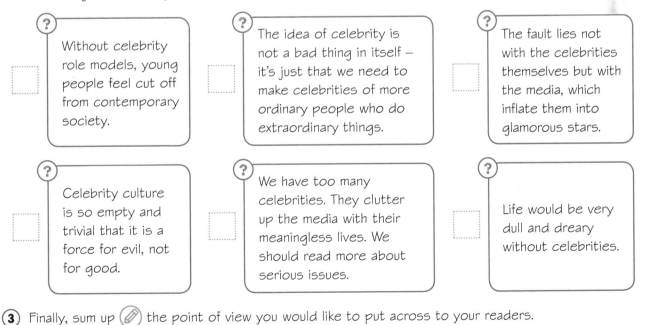

(3) Finally, sum up ✎ the point of view you would like to put across to your readers.

...................................................................................................................................................................

...................................................................................................................................................................

...................................................................................................................................................................

...................................................................................................................................................................

## ② How do I develop my ideas?

Ways of developing ideas include:

- reference to personal experience and the experience of people you know
- reference to shared knowledge and culture or other aspects of culture (the past, other countries)
- logical argument
- making an appeal to your reader's feelings or instincts.

① Think about the exam-style question on page 11 and the key phrases 'we all need' and 'purposeful life'. Then look at the questions below which one student noted in a plan for their writing task. Rank ✎ them from 1 to 6 according to how well you think they address the key phrases in the question, where 1 is 'exceptionally well' and 6 is 'not very well at all'.

| How have celebrities affected me? For better or worse? | How have celebrities affected people I know? Positively or negatively? | Do I know people who have not been much affected by celebrities? What sort of people are they and could their experience reinforce my argument? |
|---|---|---|
| ☐ | ☐ | ☐ |
| Can the past help me to see things in a different light? (e.g. name two or three past celebrities; impact at the time; contrast with today's culture) | Can I base my argument on widely held perceptions of the world? (e.g. 'modern culture is not ideal', or 'popular culture cannot please everyone') | Can I find two or three problems associated with the influence of celebrity role models, then discuss possible solutions? |
| ☐ | ☐ | ☐ |

② Now write ✎ three introductory sentences for three paragraphs based on the ideas you ranked highest in the activity above.

a ...............................................................................................................................

...............................................................................................................................

...............................................................................................................................

b ...............................................................................................................................

...............................................................................................................................

...............................................................................................................................

c ...............................................................................................................................

...............................................................................................................................

...............................................................................................................................

## 3 How do I plan an effective conclusion?

Endings are often the weakest part of student responses, but they are important because they are the final impression the reader takes away. The better your planning and your sense of direction throughout, the stronger your conclusion is likely to be.

(1) Imagine you are thinking about how to conclude your response to the exam-style question on page 11. Which of the following possibilities would you be most likely to choose? Tick ✓ the boxes that correspond to your choice(s). It is possible to combine two, or even three, of them.

☐ A surprising but relevant fact, e.g. There have been a number of deranged individuals obsessed with celebrities...

☐ A rhetorical question for the reader, e.g. How do we choose the right role models?

☐ An anecdote, e.g. A friend of mine idolised...

☐ A strong final statement, e.g. Famous people can inspire, but they can also corrupt, just as fame itself can corrupt.

☐ A positive note, e.g. The right people can inspire us to great things.

☐ An appeal for a change in the way people think, e.g. Above all we must learn to think for ourselves, not allow celebrities to do the thinking for us or, even worse, persuade us to sidestep the thinking altogether.

☐ A broad-based, impersonal sentence, e.g. One can only hope that...

☐ A warning for the future, perhaps containing a vivid image, e.g. Otherwise our culture is likely to find its own level of least resistance, like water running into a marsh.

☐ A link with the opening, e.g. So, to return to the opening question – no, we don't all need celebrities...

(2) Now try writing ✐ two possible conclusions yourself, using the above options to help you.

Conclusion 1: ........................................................................................

.............................................................................................................

.............................................................................................................

.............................................................................................................

.............................................................................................................

Conclusion 2: ........................................................................................

.............................................................................................................

.............................................................................................................

.............................................................................................................

.............................................................................................................

.............................................................................................................

# Sample response

To generate ideas when you are writing to present a viewpoint, you need to:

- focus on the key words and phrases in the task
- think about two or three possible viewpoints on the topic
- think of some useful evidence (factual accuracy is not important)
- review methods of presenting a viewpoint, such as anecdote, quotation or rhetorical question.

Now look again at the exam-style writing task on page 11.

Look at one student's plan written in response to the task.

---

*My viewpoint:* Celebrities can be a big distraction – famous people from the past can be some of the best role models if we choose the right ones.

| Points | Evidence |
|---|---|
| Celebrities (one category of 'famous people') can lead us astray. | Wild pop stars could lead children to unhealthy experimentation with lifestyle choices, e.g. sex and drugs. Also they can lend authority to bad behaviour. |
| We should draw our role models from the past as well as the present – culture is partly a matter of transmitting tradition. | Writers might look to novelists and poets such as Dickens and Steinbeck, Yeats and T S Eliot, or even Shakespeare, for inspiration, just as they have in the past. |
| Role models we choose from the present should not all be famous – they might be brilliant but not well known, or they might be in some ways fairly ordinary. | What about musicians who are good but not famous? Professionals who are very good at what they do? People who do something unusual/heroic such as going to help in a country hit by disaster? |
| We don't always appreciate that people who act unselfishly are often the most admirable. | A man in Germany risked his life to get someone out of a burning car, which exploded soon afterwards. |

---

(1) Annotate ✏ the plan to label and comment on effective features such as good arguments for, possible arguments against, and useful evidence.

(2) Add ✏ anything else you can think of that would improve this plan. Use the space below to list your ideas.

.................................................................................

.................................................................................

.................................................................................

.................................................................................

# Your turn!

You are now going to plan your response to this exam-style task.

'We all need famous role models – they inspire us to pursue a purposeful life.'

Write an article for a national broadsheet newspaper expressing your views on this topic.

(40 marks)

(1) What is the main point of view that you want to get across in your article? Write 🖉 a sentence or two summarising your standpoint.

..........................................................................................................................................................

..........................................................................................................................................................

..........................................................................................................................................................

(2) What pros and cons will you write about? What evidence can you use to support your opinion? Make a note 🖉 of them below.

The pros are...




The cons are...




My view is justified because...




(3) Now write 🖉 your response to the above exam-style question on paper.

# Review your skills

## Check up

Review your response to the exam-style question on page 15. Tick ✓ the column to show how well you think you have done each of the following.

|  | Not quite ✓ | Nearly there ✓ | Got it! ✓ |
|---|---|---|---|
| identified my intention | ☐ | ☐ | ☐ |
| developed my ideas | ☐ | ☐ | ☐ |
| planned an effective conclusion | ☐ | ☐ | ☐ |

Look over all your work in this unit.

Note down 🖉 the three most important things that might help you to plan a response that will convey your point of view.

1. ...........................................................................................................

2. ...........................................................................................................

3. ...........................................................................................................

## Need more practice?

Plan your response to the exam-style task below.

**Exam-style question**

'Computer games have changed the nature of teenage boys – and not for the better.'

Write an article for a newspaper in which you explain your point of view on this statement.

(40 marks)

How confident do you feel about each of these **skills?** Colour 🖉 in the bars.

**❶ How do I identify my intention?**

**❷ How do I develop my ideas?**

**❸ How do I plan an effective conclusion?**

# ③ Structuring your ideas – narrative and descriptive writing

This unit will help you learn how to structure your ideas for a narrative or descriptive writing task. The skills you will build are to:

- shape your creative writing
- structure your creative writing for impact
- take on a persona in your creative writing.

In the exam, you will be asked to tackle writing tasks such as the one below. This unit will prepare you to write your own response to this question.

> **Exam-style question**
>
> You are going to enter a creative writing competition.
>
> Your entry will be judged by a panel of people of your own age.
>
> **Either:** Write a description suggested by this picture.
>
> **Or:** Write a story about a time when you came under a bad influence.
>
>
>
> (40 marks)

The three key questions in the **skills boosts** will help you to structure your ideas for a narrative and descriptive writing task.

① **How do I shape my creative writing?**   ② **How do I structure my creative writing for impact?**   ③ **How do I take on a persona in my creative writing?**

Look at one student's plan for the narrative writing task on page 18.

Write a story about a time when you came under a bad influence.

- Atmosphere at home: my mother notices something is wrong and asks over breakfast
- I say nothing and don't eat – push part of breakfast onto sister's plate
- Getting out of house; leave without saying goodbye and head to join Tom's gang; anxiety/excitement
- Build-up to my turn to run in front of cars; my turn announced
- Head to spot on road round corner
- Waiting – tension
- Focus on fear – T pushes me into the road
- Car brakes hard
- Angry man gets out

(**1**) Think about whether this story plan shows:

- the way this story begins, develops and ends ☐
- the characters and how they develop. ☐

    Put a tick (✓) or a cross (✗) in each box to give your opinion.

(**2**) Note (✎) your thoughts in the table below about:

(**a**) what is effective about this story plan

(**b**) what could be improved – add some of your own ideas.

| What is effective about the plan? ✎ | What ideas could you add to improve it? ✎ |
|---|---|
| | |

# 1 How do I shape my creative writing?

In a very short story, it is best to keep the plot simple. You will probably be writing only six or seven paragraphs, and you need to focus on the quality of your writing, rather than trying to cram in too many characters or events.

Below are three plot ideas in response to the narrative writing task on page 18.

**A**
A young man in a dystopian society goes to a meeting about a rebellion, then is forced to escape when an attack occurs.

**B**
A boy leaves his mother on holiday to explore, sees boys diving off rocks and tries to copy them, with some success but some pain, too.

**C**
A robot 'wakes up', and discovers that the man who he thinks of as his 'father' is his enemy, although his 'mother' is his friend.

Think about the types of writing you can use: first-person narrative or omniscient narrator; description of character's thoughts and feelings (very important for intelligent storytelling); dialogue; background information; flashback.

To focus on the overall shape of your story, you need to think also about the **Exposition**, **Conflict**, **Climax** and **Resolution**.

(1) Write ✏ a plan for one of the plot ideas above and use the table to organise your ideas. Plan about six points (so you could have more than one point in each section of the table). Include not only what is happening but also how you will relate the events and select key ideas that will produce maximum impact.

| | |
|---|---|
| Exposition (introduction to character and situation) | |
| Conflict (central problem) | |
| Climax (crisis caused by problem) | |
| Resolution (outcome) | |

(2) Look at your plan. Number the points/section to reorder them for maximum impact. Write ✏ a full plan on paper outlining the content and style of each paragraph.

**Unit 3 Structuring your ideas – narrative and descriptive writing** 19

## 2 How do I structure my creative writing for impact?

The opening is very important to any piece of writing; it should establish character and setting, and also suggest what issue the story will tackle. If the task is descriptive, it is still a good idea to involve character, but there should be a greater concentration on mood and atmosphere.

Read these three story openings; each student uses a different approach. The first two are descriptive tasks, the third is narrative.

### Student A

I'd seen it before under cloudless sunny skies, and of course the bright colours and the whole pathetic fallacy of summer weather made those massive towers look almost benign. But today was darker, more dramatic – and more appropriate for those monsters.

### Student B

Although it was the middle of the broiling Australian summer, it was raining hard. Through the mud-spattered window of the car I watched my blurred world go by: I could just glimpse dusty reddish earth through the motorway barriers. I was leaving my twelve-year-old self behind, although it was none of my doing.

### Student C

Up until that winter I had been outgoing, confident, some might have said happy. There had been nothing, really, to make me unhappy other than the typical disappointments of a competitive teenager who doesn't win everything he wants to. But that's hardly a big deal, is it?

(1) Tick ⊘ your favourite from the openings above and note down ✎ how it engages your interest and how it makes you feel.

.................................................................................................................

.................................................................................................................

.................................................................................................................

(2) For each opening, complete the following table:

| | Which is the most effective phrase? ✎ | Why is the phrase effective? ✎ |
|---|---|---|
| A | | |
| B | | |
| C | | |

(3) Finally, on a separate piece of paper, write ✎ your own opening to one of the tasks on page 17.

# ③ How do I take on a persona in my creative writing?

Much of the character of fiction depends upon the persona or voice created by the author – think of famous narrators like Huckleberry Finn, or Robinson Crusoe. It is well worth thinking about the persona you wish to create before you begin your story or description.

Here are some types of persona, with an example of each voice. Note  one advantage and one disadvantage you think you might find in using this persona.

**A Teenage/young adult colloquial**

> I was chatting away to Susie when suddenly she sees some guy, some freak more like, on the other side of the room. So she waltzes over to him and starts to schmooze away.

Advantage: ..............................................................................................................................

..............................................................................................................................

Disadvantage: ..............................................................................................................................

**B Omniscient well-educated** (the style of most classic and much modern literary fiction)

> Charlie had been living in a little town in Shropshire for four years before coming to Birmingham: it had taken him a while to get used to his new big-city surroundings.

Advantage: ..............................................................................................................................

..............................................................................................................................

Disadvantage: ..............................................................................................................................

**C First-person unreliable** (i.e. we cannot trust that everything they say is true, for reasons that should become clear)

> My father had got it so totally wrong, I knew that immediately. He was always on the defensive in arguments with my mother. He couldn't see... And he didn't understand me either...

Advantage: ..............................................................................................................................

..............................................................................................................................

Disadvantage: ..............................................................................................................................

**D Free indirect style** (third-person narrative that also uses the character's inward thoughts)

> He turned at the lights on to the road that led north. Life was going to be better for him from now on. He would go and see Sam.

Advantage: ..............................................................................................................................

..............................................................................................................................

Disadvantage: ..............................................................................................................................

# Sample response

To structure descriptive writing effectively, you should:

- consider ways to engage your reader from the very first sentence
- include a character but focus more on mood and atmosphere
- use techniques to vary the perspective or the timeframe.

To structure narrative writing effectively, you should:

- consider ways of engaging your reader straight away
- use a typical story structure such as **Exposition – Conflict – Climax – Resolution**
- think about different writing styles and narrative perspectives
- create a satisfying ending.

**Exam-style question**

Write a story about a time when you came under a bad influence.

| Exposition | Conflict | Climax | Resolution |
|---|---|---|---|
| Sam comes down to breakfast – knowing that his mother is picking up his tense mood; leaves the house. | Goes to rendezvous with friends – his turn to play 'chicken': the others take him to the best spot and watch him. | He runs out into the road when the leader shouts 'Go!' but doesn't make it to the other side in time – car brakes hard just in front of him. | Friends run off. Sam has to face the angry driver alone. |

(1) Look carefully at **Exposition**. Write ✐ the first sentence or two of the story, aiming to make it as engaging as possible.

........................................................................................................

........................................................................................................

........................................................................................................

........................................................................................................

........................................................................................................

(2) Now look carefully at **Resolution**. Can you think of a more satisfying ending to the story? Write ✐ a sentence or two explaining your ideas.

........................................................................................................

........................................................................................................

........................................................................................................

........................................................................................................

........................................................................................................

........................................................................................................

# Your turn!

You are now going to plan your response to this exam-style task.

**Exam-style question**

You are going to enter a creative writing competition.

Your entry will be judged by a panel of people of your own age.

**Either:** Write a description suggested by this picture.

**Or:** Write a story about a time when you came under a bad influence.

(40 marks)

1. Note ✎ down all the ideas you will use in your plan for the **descriptive writing task**.

2. Note ✎ down all the ideas you will use in your plan for the **narrative writing task**.

3. Decide which task you will plan in full – the descriptive writing or the narrative writing task.

   a. Think about the opening of your story or description. How will you engage the reader straight away? Note ✎ your ideas below.

   b. How will your story or description end? Note ✎ one or two possibilities below.

4. Now plan ✎ your response to the above exam-style question on paper.

# Review your skills

## Check up

Review your response to the exam-style question on page 23. Tick  the column to show how well you think you have done each of the following.

| | Not quite | Nearly there | Got it! |
|---|---|---|---|
| shaped my creative writing | ☐ | ☐ | ☐ |
| structured my creative writing for impact | ☐ | ☐ | ☐ |
| taken on a persona in my creative writing | ☐ | ☐ | ☐ |

Look over all your work in this unit. Note down the two most important things to remember when planning a descriptive writing task.

1. .................................................................................

2. .................................................................................

Now note down the two most important things to remember when planning a narrative writing task.

1. .................................................................................

2. .................................................................................

## Need more practice?

Plan your response to the writing task from the exam-style question below that you did **not** choose in the planning activity on page 23.

### Exam-style question

You are going to enter a creative writing competition.

Your entry will be judged by a panel of people of your own age.

**Either:** Write a description suggested by this picture.

**Or:** Write a story about a time when you came under a bad influence.

(40 marks)

How confident do you feel about each of these **skills?** Colour in the bars.

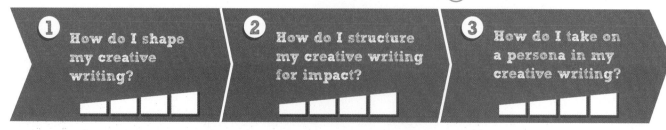

❶ How do I shape my creative writing?

❷ How do I structure my creative writing for impact?

❸ How do I take on a persona in my creative writing?

# ④ Structuring your ideas – writing to present a viewpoint

This unit will help you learn how to structure your ideas when you are writing to present a viewpoint. The skills you will build are to:

- shape your writing
- structure your writing
- develop the structure to create impact.

In the exam, you will be asked to tackle writing tasks such as the one below. This unit will prepare you to write your own response to this question.

**Exam-style question**

'Conditions in schools need to be improved.'

Write a speech to be given to parents arguing the case for this point of view.    **(40 marks)**

The three key questions in the **skills boosts** will help you to structure your ideas when you are writing to present a viewpoint.

| ① How do I shape my writing? | ② How do I structure my writing? | ③ How do I develop the structure to create impact? |

Look at one student's plan for the task on page 26.

Look carefully at the plan below. Think about the structure and content of the student's argument in response to the task on page 25.

> The first reason why conditions must improve is that a poor-quality environment leads to poor-quality attitudes and poor-quality work.
>
> They think that youngsters are too yobbish to take care of expensive resources. I say, how are children ever to learn to value such resources if they never encounter them?
>
> Are you prepared to stand up and demand that something is done?
>
> Your children are the future citizens of the state and if we want their best efforts and loyalty to the nation, we must show them when they are young that we value them.
>
> The minimum our children deserve is this: attractive...
>
> We must act now to safeguard standards and not be deflected...

(1) Does the plan have a clear and logical structure? Label ✎ the plan down the left-hand side to identify the following sections: **Introduction**, **Paragraphs 1**, **2**, **3** and **4**, **Conclusion**.

(2) Could the structure be altered to make the argument more effective? Label ✎ the plan down the right-hand side with an alternative sequence that you think might have more impact.

(3) Write ✎ a sentence or two about why you think the changes you made would improve the structure of the student's response.

...................................................................................................................................

...................................................................................................................................

...................................................................................................................................

...................................................................................................................................

(4) Can you think of any other points or argument techniques that might improve the speech? Note ✎ your ideas below.

Other points:

...................................................................................................................................

...................................................................................................................................

Other techniques:

...................................................................................................................................

...................................................................................................................................

# 1 How do I shape my writing?

When writing to argue a viewpoint, a useful strategy is to jot down more ideas than you will use – then you can select only those that will make your points most cogently. Any ideas that do not fit well with your other points should be discarded.

**Exam-style question**

'School offers the best possible preparation for the opportunities and challenges of adult life.'

Write an article for your school magazine expressing your views on this statement.     **(40 marks)**

Look at the following ideas that one student noted in a plan written in response to the exam-style question above.

> School lays the foundations for all your future achievements.
>
> School helps you create friendships that last and which help form your attitudes and character.
>
> Education prepares you for many aspects of adult life in general.
>
> Sports at school develop confidence and team-building skills.
>
> Practical subjects at school such as DT can develop useful manual and design skills.
>
> Music could lead to a lifelong hobby as well as develop real talent.
>
> Clubs and societies offer great opportunities for making friends.

(1) Which points do you think could be left out without affecting the main argument?

   (a) Put a cross (X) against **two** points that you would not include in your response.

   (b) Why did you choose to omit these particular points?

........................................................................................

........................................................................................

........................................................................................

........................................................................................

(2) Look at the points that remain.

   (a) Why did you choose to keep these particular points in your argument? What, in your opinion, makes them more effective than the points you chose to eliminate?

........................................................................................

........................................................................................

........................................................................................

........................................................................................

   (b) Which are the strongest two points of those that remain? Decide which one to use as your introduction and which one to use as your conclusion. Write 'I' and 'C' in the appropriate boxes.

## ② How do I structure my writing?

Surprising the reader can be an effective tactic in writing to present a viewpoint: you can construct a plan and then think about interesting ways of bringing it to life, to boost the impact of your message.

Here is one student's plan in response to the exam-style question on page 25.

- The first reason why conditions must improve is that a poor-quality environment leads to poor-quality attitudes and poor-quality work.

- They think that youngsters are too yobbish to take care of expensive resources. I say, how are children ever to learn to value such resources if they never encounter them?

- Are you prepared to stand up and demand that something is done?

- Your children are the future citizens of the state and if we want their best efforts and loyalty to the nation, we must show them when they are young that we value them.

- The minimum our children deserve is this: attractive...

- We must act now to safeguard standards and not be deflected...

① Which of the following techniques do you think would be suitable to use when writing to present a point of view? Circle Ⓐ any that you feel would help to enhance the student's argument.

| analogy or parallel | hyperbole | humour | onomatopeia | alliteration |

| emotive language | repetition | rhetorical question | facts and statistics |

② Choose **one** of the techniques you circled and decide which idea from the plan it could be applied to most effectively. Rewrite 🖉 the point, increasing its impact by using the technique you have chosen.

......................................................................................

......................................................................................

Another useful technique is anecdote, which often personalises the appeal of a line of argument.

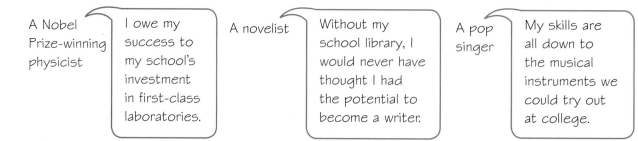

A Nobel Prize-winning physicist — I owe my success to my school's investment in first-class laboratories.

A novelist — Without my school library, I would never have thought I had the potential to become a writer.

A pop singer — My skills are all down to the musical instruments we could try out at college.

③ Use an anecdote to illustrate a point you could make about the provision of new facilities. Write 🖉 it in the space below.

Either invent an anecdote or use one you have heard before. Factual accuracy is not important; the focus is on quality of expression and language.

**How do I develop the structure to create impact?**

A strong structure in an article or speech will create an impact on the audience almost without them realising it – they will *sense* it, just as they may feel confused by a weak structure. Merging similar ideas and sequencing them logically helps to create a solid argument that might well persuade the audience to agree with your point of view.

Look again at the points one student noted when planning a response to the writing task on page 27.

> School lays the foundations for all your future achievements.
>
> School helps you to create friendships that last and help form your attitudes and character.
>
> Education prepares you for many aspects of adult life in general.
>
> Sports at school develop confidence and team-building skills.
>
> Practical subjects at school such as DT can develop useful manual and design skills.
>
> Music could lead to a lifelong hobby as well as develop real talent.
>
> Clubs and societies offer great opportunities for making friends.

(1) Could any of these ideas be merged to make a more fully developed point? Underline (A) these ideas and write (✏) the new version of the point or points in the space below.

(2) In what order would you sequence the student's points for maximum relevance and impact in your argument? Number (✏) them in the boxes provided.

Remember to give any merged points the same number to show they now belong together.

(3) Finally, think of a controversial counter-argument to the view you are expressing. Try to incorporate it into your response while at the same time counteracting it to reinforce your own opinion. (✏)

*Some people who dropped out of school might think that...* ......................................................

....................................................................................................................

....................................................................................................................

*but I believe...* ...............................................................................................

....................................................................................................................

# Sample response

To structure your writing to present a viewpoint effectively, you should include:

- an introduction that clarifies your views on the topic and engages the reader
- logically sequenced and signposted key points
- a conclusion that sums up your ideas and their benefits.

Now look again at this exam-style writing task.

**Exam-style question**

'Conditions in schools need to be improved.'

Write a speech to be given to parents arguing the case for this point of view.　　**(40 marks)**

Look at one student's response to this task.

*Introduction: Brief view on topic — why improvement is needed*

1. *Why some people think it's not worth spending all the money*

2. *What modern schools should be like*

3. *How we can try to make things change*

*Conclusion: The need to act now*

(1) What advice would you give this student to improve their plan? Note ✐ three suggestions.

Suggestion 1: .................................................................................................

.................................................................................................................

.................................................................................................................

.................................................................................................................

.................................................................................................................

Suggestion 2: .................................................................................................

.................................................................................................................

.................................................................................................................

.................................................................................................................

Suggestion 3: .................................................................................................

.................................................................................................................

.................................................................................................................

.................................................................................................................

.................................................................................................................

# Your turn!

You are now going to write your response to this exam-style task.

## Exam-style question

'Conditions in schools need to be improved.'

Write a speech to be given to parents arguing the case for this point of view. **(40 marks)**

Use the activities below to help you form your views and gather some ideas.

**(1)** Why do conditions need improving in many schools? Note 🖊 up to three reasons.

**Reason 1:** ..............................................................................................................................................

**Reason 2:** ..............................................................................................................................................

**Reason 3:** ..............................................................................................................................................

**(2)** What aspects in particular need improvement? Note 🖊 up to three points.

**Point 1:** ..............................................................................................................................................

**Point 2:** ..............................................................................................................................................

**Point 3:** ..............................................................................................................................................

**(3)** What obstacles and opposition lie in the way? Note 🖊 up to three points.

**Point 1:** ..............................................................................................................................................

**Point 2:** ..............................................................................................................................................

**Point 3:** ..............................................................................................................................................

**(4)** List 🖊 three techniques you could use to persuade your audience that something needs to be done.

**Technique 1:** ..............................................................................................................................................

**Technique 2:** ..............................................................................................................................................

**Technique 3:** ..............................................................................................................................................

**(5)** Write down 🖊 three phrases which use the techniques you listed in activity 4, and which might add a persuasive or rhetorical touch to your speech.

**Phrase 1:** ..............................................................................................................................................

**Phrase 2:** ..............................................................................................................................................

**Phrase 3:** ..............................................................................................................................................

**(5)** Now plan 🖊 your response to the above exam-style question on paper. Aim to:

- gather, merge and sequence your key points
- include some persuasive techniques, e.g. knocking down a counter-argument
- include a surprising or controversial fact or anecdote.

# Review your skills

## Check up

Review your response to the exam-style question on page 31. Tick ✓ the column to show how well you think you have done each of the following.

| | Not quite ✓ | Nearly there ✓ | Got it! ✓ |
|---|---|---|---|
| shaped your writing | ☐ | ☐ | ☐ |
| structured your writing | ☐ | ☐ | ☐ |
| developed the structure to create impact | ☐ | ☐ | ☐ |

Look over all of your work in this unit. Note down ✏ three things you should remember to do and three things you should remember not to do when structuring your writing to present a viewpoint.

DO:

1. ......................................................................................................

2. ......................................................................................................

3. ......................................................................................................

DON'T:

1. ......................................................................................................

2. ......................................................................................................

3. ......................................................................................................

## Need more practice?

Plan your response to the task below.

**Exam-style question**

'Teenagers are too often misunderstood – they are treated as a mass rather than as individuals.'

Write an article for a broadsheet newspaper in which you present your views on this statement.

(40 marks)

How confident do you feel about each of these **skills?** Colour ✏ in the bars.

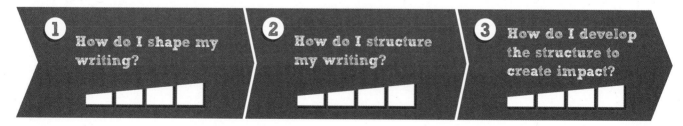

❶ **How do I shape my writing?**

❷ **How do I structure my writing?**

❸ **How do I develop the structure to create impact?**

**Communicate clearly, effectively and imaginatively with a range of vocabulary and sentence structures (AO5)**

# ⑤ Cohesion – making it clear

This unit will help you learn how to give your writing cohesion: leading the reader through your ideas by linking them clearly and fluently. The skills you will build are to:

- guide the reader through your writing

- structure paragraphs to link your ideas

- develop your ideas without repeating yourself.

In the exam, you will be asked to tackle writing tasks such as the ones below. This unit will prepare you to write your own responses to these questions.

## Paper 1

**Exam-style question**

Your school or college is asking students to contribute some creative writing for its website.

Write a story about a time when you were not happy with your surroundings.     (40 marks)

## Paper 2

**Exam-style question**

'The media wreck the lives of the famous – they make them into soulless puppets.'

Write an article for a broadsheet newspaper in which you explain your point of view on this statement.     (40 marks)

The three key questions in the **skills boosts** will help you to achieve cohesion in your writing by linking your ideas fluently and clearly.

① **How do I guide the reader through my writing?**  ② **How do I structure paragraphs to link my ideas?**  ③ **How do I develop my ideas without repeating myself?**

Look at extracts from one student's answers to the tasks above on page 34.

## Paper 1

I'd seen it before under cloudless sunny skies, and of course the bright colours and the whole pathetic fallacy of summer weather made those massive towers look almost benign. But today was darker, more dramatic. The sky was full of heavy dark grey clouds, parting in the west to let some silvery shafts of light beam down towards the towers, which were cast into a strong relief. Huge columns of grey steam poured out of the tops into the clouds above. Nearby were the great chimneys and solid blocks of the rest of the power station, the colossal generator for an entire county.

They dwarfed the trees and dominated the landscape with their sullen and brutish profiles; the plant employed hundreds, mainly men, making them its servants. Buildings do have personalities; it's not just that they are elegant or ugly or whatever – no, they exert an influence, they have an attitude. Now we were going to have to live with these ogres – our new house was half a mile away.

## Paper 2

The media feed off the famous and vice versa – they are a mutual love-hate society. Yes – they need each other – the famous inspire the media to pursue a profitable existence, and the media inspire the famous to do more and more outrageous things. That's not to say they're all bad. Just symbiotic, stuck together like conjoined twins, and craving attention for its own sake. Sounds immature? Well think about who we're talking about: a range of teenage pop idols, and behind them a whole string of kids who won't grow up. We're fascinated by them, and maybe we even love them – but does their fame ruin their lives, and do nothing for us into the bargain?

① Evaluate the fluency and clarity of the two responses. List ✎ the features in both that make a positive contribution to their cohesion.

Paper 1: ........................................................................................................

........................................................................................................

........................................................................................................

Paper 2: ........................................................................................................

........................................................................................................

........................................................................................................

② Now think about ways that both responses could be improved. Note ✎ your advice below.

Paper 1: ........................................................................................................

........................................................................................................

........................................................................................................

Paper 2: ........................................................................................................

........................................................................................................

........................................................................................................

# 1  How do I guide the reader through my writing?

You will already be familiar with the adverbials most commonly used to **sequence** writing, but it is possible to limit the use of the obvious signposts by using connectives which are less formulaic, more precise and more varied.

**(1)** Write down ✏ eight common adverbials which help to sequence points either **in order of importance** or **chronologically.**

......................................  ......................................  ......................................  ......................................

......................................  ......................................  ......................................  ......................................

Other adverbials can guide the reader by signalling more complex relationships between ideas. For example, they can indicate:

**contradiction,** e.g.
| however | on the other hand | nonetheless |

**exemplification,** e.g.
| for instance | for example |

**cause and effect,** e.g.
| consequently | therefore | as a result |

**elaboration,** e.g.
| in other words | that is to say | put simply |

**emphasis,** e.g.
| above all | indeed | significantly |

**addition,** e.g.
| moreover | furthermore | additionally |

**illustration,** e.g.
| namely | specifically | explicitly |

**qualification,** e.g.
| of course | in point of fact | sometimes |

**(2)** Look at the sentences below. Add ✏ appropriate adverbials in the blank spaces to link them clearly and logically.

> *Every month, we hear stories of yet more meaningless adventures involving celebrities.*
> *................................, you might think that the public would be heartily sick of them.*
> *................................, the media have found ingenious ways of ensuring that there is an endless supply of them.*
> *................................, the appetite for such stories never seems to diminish.*

**(3)** Adverbials can be placed at different points in a sentence without affecting the meaning. Choose **one** of the sentences above. Rewrite ✏ it, moving the adverbial to a different position.

......................................................................................................................................

......................................................................................................................................

## ② How do I structure paragraphs to link my ideas?

Thinking about the first sentence of a paragraph, and how it links back to the last sentence of the previous one, will help to give your writing greater fluency and coherence.

Look at the following extract from a student response to a descriptive task. Focus particularly on the words in **bold** type.

> Nearby were the **great chimneys** and **solid blocks** of the rest of the power station, the colossal generator for an entire county.
>
> **They** dwarfed the trees and dominated the landscape with their sullen and brutish profiles. As I looked up at **these monoliths**, I felt obscurely intimidated...

**①** Explain ✏ how the second paragraph links back to the first in this response.

.............................................................................................................................

.............................................................................................................................

More complex links between paragraphs can develop through **using contrast**, for example by taking a step forwards or backwards in **time**, moving the action to a different **place**, changing the protagonist's **state of mind** or capturing a different **mood**.

> The sounds of vehicles awakening rumbled along every alley and crevice, filling trains and buses as they zipped away out towards the suburbs. All but the least penetrable of dwellings and the deepest of sleepers, of whom he was for the time being one, knew of the ceasing of the great city's slumber.
>
> The screeching of the train jerked him awake. Sluggishly rubbing his eyes, he gazed from his pillow towards the window.

**②** Underline (A) the words in the first and second paragraphs that form a cohesive link in this response.

**③** Rewrite ✏ the first sentence of the second paragraph twice, using two different linking techniques.

ⓐ ...........................................................................................................................

ⓑ ...........................................................................................................................

**④** Underline (A) the linking words in each of your new versions.

**⑤** ⓐ Which of the three versions of the sentence reads most clearly and fluently? Circle (A) it below.

| Original version | My version ⓐ | My version ⓑ |

ⓑ Explain ✏ why you think this.

.............................................................................................................................

.............................................................................................................................

## ③ How do I develop my ideas without repeating myself?

You may be aware already of the need to avoid endless repetition of key words from the question in your answer but skilful writers can achieve so much more than this; you should aim for a natural-sounding variation in expression to keep your reader engaged and the argument moving forward.

Read the following extract from one student's response to the Paper 2-style question on page 33. Note the repeated words in bold type.

> The media feed off the famous and vice versa – they are a mutual **love**–hate society. Yes – they need each other – the **famous** inspire the **media** to pursue a profitable existence, and the **media inspire** the **famous** to do more and more outrageous things. That's not to say they're all **bad**. Just symbiotic, stuck together like conjoined twins, and craving attention for its own sake. Sounds immature? Well, think about who we're talking about: a range of teenage pop idols, and behind them a whole string of kids who won't grow up. We're fascinated by them, and some of us even **love** them – but does their fame ruin their lives, and have a **bad** effect on us into the bargain?

① List  some more precise synonyms that could replace the repeated words below to display a greater variety of vocabulary in the response.

| famous .......................... | famous .......................... |
|---|---|

| inspire .......................... | love .......................... | bad .......................... |
|---|---|---|

Now look at how a more skilful student has used repetition sparingly to their advantage, achieving a subtle variation of expression while maintaining the flow and coherence of their argument.

> Ofsted reports repeatedly expose the grim quality of Britain's school premises. Cluttered classrooms, foul toilet facilities and inadequate outdoor space are all too commonly reported: over 60% of schools operate out of shoddy buildings. It is high time that the school authorities took action.
>
> Some people think that it is not worth providing decent facilities for children. They think that youngsters are too yobbish to take care of expensive resources. I say, how are children ever to learn to value such resources if they never encounter them?

② Complete ⊘ the following sentences to explain how the second paragraph links back to the first and then develops the argument in this response.

**The first sentence:** ..............................................................................................

.....................................................................................................................

**The second sentence:** ...........................................................................................

.....................................................................................................................

**The third sentence:** ..............................................................................................

.....................................................................................................................

# Sample response

To make your writing as clear and fluent as possible, you should try to:

- use adverbials to make links and guide the reader
- link the first sentence of a paragraph back to the last of the previous one
- avoid excessive repetition in the way you express yourself.

Now look at this exam-style writing task.

**Exam-style question**

Your school or college is asking students to contribute to a creative writing competition.

Write about a time when you were in a difficult situation.

(40 marks)

Read this sample answer.

One of the worst situations in my life happened a year ago: it was when I had to look after my grandfather quite a lot of the time because I was living in his house doing my GCSEs (because we have moved house but I didn't want to change schools). It was a time of transition for me, working part-time and studying as well. The problem was not that he was ill, but that he was very forgetful, perhaps had a touch of dementia; and also that he was more prone to be critical and awkward than he had been.

Well I managed to handle the situation – the shopping, the organisation, the somewhat difficult conversations, with some vital help from my boyfriend, who visited often and talked to him about sport. It was difficult, though, sometimes talking to him, not just because he would forget so many things, but because his moods were unpredictable and if he was in a bad mood he could say the most hurtful things. I knew he didn't mean some of the things he said – not really – but it was very difficult to deal with all the same.

(1) How would you improve the cohesion of this answer?

  a Underline (A) any parts of the text that you think could be expressed more clearly and fluently.

  b Rewrite (✎) the sentences you have marked, or the entire text, thinking especially about:
    - using adverbials
    - making more links
    - avoiding repetition.

# Your turn!

Choose one of the two exam-style tasks that you saw at the beginning of this unit.

## Paper 1

**Exam-style question**

Your school or college is asking students to contribute some creative writing for its website.

Write a story about a time when you were not happy with your surroundings.　　(40 marks)

## Paper 2

**Exam-style question**

'The media wreck the lives of the famous – they make them into soulless puppets.'

Write an article for a broadsheet newspaper in which you explain your point of view on this statement.　　(40 marks)

Use the activities below to help you to identify your views and gather some ideas.

(1) Think about all the different points you might include in your response. Note (✎) them in the space below.

(2) (a) Choose the ideas you will focus on in the first two or three paragraphs of your response. Tick them. (✓)

(b) Number (✎) your chosen ideas in the order in which you will use them.

(3) Now write (✎) the first two or three paragraphs of your response to your chosen task on paper, thinking carefully about:

- using adverbials to link your ideas and guide the reader
- structuring paragraphs carefully
- avoiding repetition by varying the forms of key words or replacing them with synonyms.

# Review your skills

**Check up**

Review your response to the exam-style question on page 39. Tick ✓ the column to show how well you think you have done each of the following.

|  | Not quite ✓ | Nearly there ✓ | Got it! ✓ |
|---|---|---|---|
| guided the reader through my writing | ☐ | ☐ | ☐ |
| structured paragraphs to link my ideas | ☐ | ☐ | ☐ |
| developed my ideas without repeating myself | ☐ | ☐ | ☐ |

Look over all of your work in this unit. Note down ✎ three things you should remember to do to give your writing cohesion and three things you should remember not to do.

DO:

1. ................................................................

2. ................................................................

3. ................................................................

DON'T:

1. ................................................................

2. ................................................................

3. ................................................................

## Need more practice?

Write a response to the other question on page 39, or tackle the question below.

**Exam-style question**

Describe a time when you were given a special responsibility.

How confident do you feel about each of these **skills?** Colour ✎ in the bars.

**1** How do I guide the reader through my writing?

**2** How do I structure paragraphs to link my ideas?

**3** How do I develop my ideas without repeating myself?

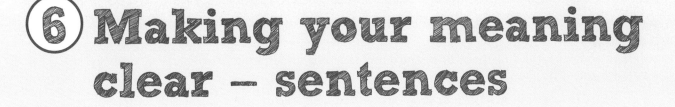

# ⑥ Making your meaning clear – sentences

This unit will help you learn how to use varied sentence structures to clarify meaning. The skills you will build are to:

- use single-clause sentences to make your meaning clear
- experiment with sentence structure to make your meaning clear
- use advanced punctuation to make your meaning clear.

In the exams, you will be asked to tackle writing tasks such as the ones below. This unit will prepare you to write your own response to these questions.

## Paper 1

**Exam-style question**

Your college or school is asking students to contribute some writing to its newsletter.

Describe a time when you suffered a loss or a disappointment.

(40 marks)

You could write about:
- the loss of a friend
- the death of a pet
- the disappointment of a broken promise.

Your response could be real or imagined.

## Paper 2

**Exam-style question**

'Young people have never before had such a wealth of opportunities laid out before them.'

Write an article for a broadsheet newspaper explaining your views on this statement.

(40 marks)

In your article, you could:
- consider what life chances young people have now that their parents did not
- consider whether greater opportunities also involve greater pressures
- suggest positive approaches young people could take towards their future prospects.

The three key questions in the **skills boosts** will help you to make your meaning clear.

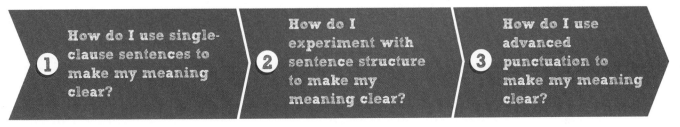

① How do I use single-clause sentences to make my meaning clear?

② How do I experiment with sentence structure to make my meaning clear?

③ How do I use advanced punctuation to make my meaning clear?

Look at extracts from two students' answers to the tasks on the next page.

Look carefully at these extracts from two students' responses to the exam-style writing tasks on page 41.

## Paper 1

He wandered around the town in the rain hoping it might distract him somehow from his misery. He didn't know how to go on with this life, not without her. He paused in front of a shop. The water-splattered window in front of him held various antiques – polished old tables and chairs. The reflected image of the wet street behind him showed a world full of life: busy and purposeful. The bitter wind must be only a few degrees above zero. His legs, hands and head were shivering fiercely as if symptoms of some dreadful illness. He looked up into the wide and misty mirror and saw nothing but a boy who might as well forget to live, who would end up homeless and hopeless. Things looked so bleak. Every second, he thought, led him closer to some kind of oblivion.

## Paper 2

Youth is a time of endless opportunities, and pressures in plentiful supply. They are academic, social, economic, all coming at us in varied forms and intensity; and beyond our little personal lives there are other pressures more massive – national and global. We are bombarded by waves of pressure from all sides. We have enough to deal with for a lifetime.

But – hang on – there have never been so many ways of making our own decisions and finding our own little path through the time-deadlined-maze. We are not in a hothouse or a cooker, but a landscape with many different routes through it. We can choose. We can live in our own little worlds with our friends if we like – up to a point; and we can find out about all the different ways there are of making a life, of earning money, in a world which has never presented so much variety of opportunity for young people. Think about it: the youth culture of the 60s has become a permanent but ever-changing feature, spawning myriad enterprises.

(1) (a) Which of the responses above is more clearly written? Tick it ✓ and give a brief reason 🖊 why you think this.

  ☐ Paper 1 – ......................................................................................

  ☐ Paper 2 – ......................................................................................

(b) Which is more fluently written? Tick it ✓ and give a brief reason 🖊 why you think this.

  ☐ Paper 1 – ......................................................................................

  ☐ Paper 2 – ......................................................................................

(2) (a) Identify 🖊 two strong features of the sentences in the Paper 1 response.

  Feature 1: ......................................................................................

  Feature 2: ......................................................................................

(b) Identify 🖊 two strong features of the sentences in the Paper 2 response.

  Feature 1: ......................................................................................

  Feature 2: ......................................................................................

(3) Choose one of the responses and think about what improvements could be made to the sentence structure in terms of clarity and fluency. Make notes 🖊 below.

......................................................................................

......................................................................................

## 1 How do I use single-clause sentences to make my meaning clear?

The simple single-clause construction is often the most powerful tool in a writer's toolbox and, used sparingly, can increase clarity and impact.

**1** Re-read the two responses opposite, then look at the following sentences taken from them. What is effective about these sentences in their context? Write 🖉 brief notes about each of them.

**a** Things looked so bleak. ................................................................

....................................................................................................

**b** We are bombarded by waves of pressure from all sides. ..............

....................................................................................................

**c** We can choose. ........................................................................

....................................................................................................

**d** Think about it... .......................................................................

....................................................................................................

**2** Read the following sentence, then reduce 🖉 it to about ten words.

We're taking our minds off the fact that we should be revising for our exams if we don't want to spend the rest of our lives sleeping in a bin.

....................................................................................................

**3** **a** Write 🖉 a single-clause sentence summarising your feelings at the end of one of your paragraphs in a response you might write to the Paper 1 task.

*Try to avoid unnecessary modification by adjectives and adverbs.*

....................................................................................................

....................................................................................................

**b** Write 🖉 a single-clause sentence which emphasises part of your argument for a response you might write to the Paper 2 task.

*Remember that the most powerful arguments often use very simple language.*

....................................................................................................

....................................................................................................

**c** Are you happy with the sentences you have written? ✓

☐ Yes  ☐ No  ☐ Partly

*You could add alliteration, or condense it further, or replace the verb with a stronger, more dynamic alternative.*

**d** Redraft 🖉 one of the sentences to make it more emphatic.

....................................................................................................

....................................................................................................

## ② How do I experiment with sentence structure to make my meaning clear?

Varying your sentence structure using interesting techniques can help to clarify meaning, as well as showing your skills as a writer and thereby engaging the reader with your message.

Contrary to what many believe, it is perfectly acceptable to begin a sentence with 'and' or 'but'.

This technique can be an effective way of highlighting meaning, as shown in this example from the sample response to the Paper 2 task.

> *But – hang on – there have never been so many ways of making our own decisions…*

Here it is bolder still in its effect, because the word 'but' opens a new paragraph.

① Why do you think this technique, as long as it is used sparingly, might be effective in making meaning clear? Write 🖉 your thoughts below.

.................................................................................................................................

.................................................................................................................................

Parallel or contrasting structures within or between sentences help to focus the reader's attention on the writer's meaning. A popular technique with skilful writers is **anaphora**: beginning successive clauses or sentences with the same word or phrase.

Look at this example from the same Paper 2 response.

> *We can choose. We can live in our own little worlds with our friends if we like – up to a point; and we can find out about…*

② ⓐ What is the effect in terms of meaning of repeating the 'we + verb' structure in this way? Note 🖉 your ideas below.

.................................................................................................................................

.................................................................................................................................

ⓑ Write 🖉 a sentence of your own using this technique in response to the same task.

.................................................................................................................................

To underline meaning, it can be useful to begin a paragraph with a **verb-led subordinate clause**, such as 'Moving on to another point, …', or 'To illustrate this, we can look at…'. A command verb, such as 'Stop for a moment to consider…', is a simple but powerful persuasive device, directly addressing the audience to demand they pay attention to the writer's meaning.

③ Write 🖉 two sentences which begin with:

ⓐ a subordinate clause starting with a present participle (verb ending in -ing) or an infinitive ('to' + verb)

.................................................................................................................................

.................................................................................................................................

ⓑ a command verb.

.................................................................................................................................

.................................................................................................................................

## ③ How do I use advanced punctuation to make my meaning clear?

Punctuation, especially more advanced punctuation, can be a great help in varying sentence structure and clarifying meaning.

**Colons** are commonly used to introduce lists, but in descriptive or persuasive writing they can be much more versatile than this. For example, they can follow a general statement to present more specific detail, e.g.

> *There are three reasons why we should build a new sports block: the present building is inadequate, demand is growing and we will get a grant to help.*

They may also introduce an explanation of, or give a reason for, what has gone before, e.g.

> *I don't think you should go: it isn't safe any more.*

① Choose one of the writing tasks on page 41. Write ✐ a sentence that you might use in your response, using a colon in one of the above ways, to clarify meaning.

..................................................................................................................................................

..................................................................................................................................................

**Semi-colons** are used where you could use a full stop, but wish to indicate that the two sentences are very closely linked. Often there is a balancing effect between two similar or two opposite ideas, which underlines meaning and gives pattern and rhythm, e.g.

> *The rowing team won gold; the fencing team won silver.*

> *Television is, at times, entertaining; it can also be corrupting.*

② Write ✐ two sentences in response to the other task on page 41, using a semi-colon

ⓐ to separate complementary ideas

..................................................................................................................................................

..................................................................................................................................................

ⓑ to separate antithetical ideas.

..................................................................................................................................................

..................................................................................................................................................

The **single dash** is useful when you want to add something to your sentence, after a break that is less decisive than a full stop. We do it often in speech without realising it, e.g.

> *We can live in our own little worlds with our friends if we like – up to a point.*

What comes after the single dash has the effect of an explanatory afterthought, of the kind we might use in discussion, to make our meaning clear.

③ Write a sentence of your own using a single dash to clarify meaning, in response to either of the writing tasks on page 41.

..................................................................................................................................................

# Sample response

To make your meaning clear, you need to craft carefully structured sentences, thinking about:

- using single-clause sentences
- experimenting with sentence structure
- using advanced punctuation.

Look again at this exam-style question, and the extract from one student's response below.

**Exam-style question**

'Young people have never before had such a wealth of opportunities laid out before them.'

Write an article for a broadsheet newspaper explaining your views on this statement.

(40 marks)

---

It seems to me that teenagers are under far too much pressure from the press and social media in their lives to take advantage of any golden opportunities that may come their way. I mean, how often do you read of teenagers making people's lives miserable – teachers, parents, the general public – even each other through bullying online?

Teenagers are thought to be deliberate risk-takers, so they should be open to new experiences and able to cope with them, but the fact is that experts say that the correct way to see them is as people doing lots of things for the first time and therefore bound to make some mistakes (some of which will inevitably result in serious injury or death).

The thing is that it's not teenagers themselves – I mean their moral selves if you like – that are to blame. Experts have shown that there is an increase in risk-taking, peer influence and self-consciousness. So it is more the state of being a teenager that is to blame for their mistakes. This inevitably leads to a failure to grasp how lucky they are to have so many more exciting life-chances on offer than their parents had.

---

(1) How would you improve the fluency and clarity of this response?

**a** Underline (A) any parts of the text that you feel could be expressed more clearly and fluently.

**b** Adjust (✐) the text above, or rewrite it on paper, thinking about:
- using single-clause sentences to make your meaning clear
- experimenting with sentence structure to make your meaning clear
- using advanced punctuation to make your meaning clear.

# Your turn!

Choose one of these two exam-style tasks from the beginning of this unit.

> **Exam-style question**
>
> .Your college or school is asking students to contribute some writing to its newsletter.
>
> Describe a time when you suffered a loss or a disappointment. **(40 marks)**

> **Exam-style question**
>
> 'Young people have never before had such a wealth of opportunities laid out before them.'
>
> Write an article for a broadsheet newspaper explaining your views on this statement. **(40 marks)**

You are going to **plan** and **write** the first two or three paragraphs of your response, focusing on sentence structure.

**1** Think about all the different ideas you might include in your response. Note ✐ them in the space below.

**2 a** Choose the ideas that you will focus on in the opening two or three paragraphs of your response. Tick them. ✓

    **b** Number ✐ your chosen ideas in the order you will use them.

**3** Now write ✐ the first two or three paragraphs of your response to your chosen task on paper, thinking carefully about:

- using single-clause sentences to make your meaning clear
- experimenting with sentence structure to make your meaning clear
- using advanced punctuation to make your meaning clear.

# Review your skills

## Check up

Review your response to the exam-style question on page 47. Tick ✓ the column to show how well you think you have done each of the following.

| | Not quite ✓ | Nearly there ✓ | Got it! ✓ |
|---|---|---|---|
| used single-clause sentences to make my meaning clear | ☐ | ☐ | ☐ |
| experimented with sentence structure to make my meaning clear | ☐ | ☐ | ☐ |
| used advanced punctuation to make my meaning clear | ☐ | ☐ | ☐ |

Look over all of your work in this unit. Note down 🖉 three things you should do to make your meaning as clear as possible.

1. ...................................................................................................................

2. ...................................................................................................................

3. ...................................................................................................................

## Need more practice?

Have a go at the exam-style question below:

### Exam-style question

'Technologies such as mobile phones and computers are useful, but we use them too much. They are taking over our lives.'

Write an article for a newspaper in which you explain your point of view on this statement.

(40 marks)

How confident do you feel about each of these **skills?** Colour 🖉 in the bars.

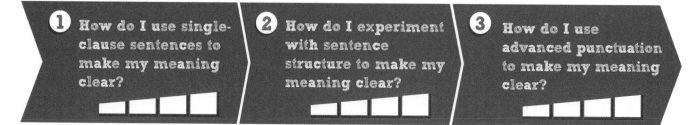

1 How do I use single-clause sentences to make my meaning clear?

2 How do I experiment with sentence structure to make my meaning clear?

3 How do I use advanced punctuation to make my meaning clear?

# (7) Writing paragraphs and sentences to create impact

This unit will help you learn how to write paragraphs and sentences that create impact. The skills you will build are to:

- structure paragraphs that engage the reader
- experiment with sentence structure to create impact
- use advanced punctuation to create impact.

In the exam, you will be asked to tackle writing tasks such as the ones below. This unit will prepare you to write your own response to one of these questions.

## Paper 1

**Exam-style question**

Write a description suggested by this picture.

(40 marks)

## Paper 2

**Exam-style question**

'Television is, on the whole, a waste of time.'

Write an article for a broadsheet newspaper explaining your opinion of this statement.   **(40 marks)**

The three key questions in the **skills boosts** will help you to write paragraphs and sentences to create impact.

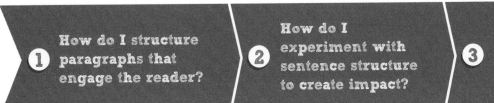

1. How do I structure paragraphs that engage the reader?

2. How do I experiment with sentence structure to create impact?

3. How do I use advanced punctuation to create impact?

Look at the extracts from one student's answer to the task on page 50.

Look at the extract below from one student's response to the descriptive task.

**Exam-style question**

Write a description suggested by this picture.

(40 marks)

> Brush fires had started in the heat after months of drought. The winds blowing in off the desert were the catalyst for the all-devouring disaster – they blew stronger, blowing the fires like bellows, until firestorms were erupting in the nearby hills. The winds accelerated up to a hundred miles an hour in the Sacramento valley. People talked of flames a hundred feet high, of birds suddenly bursting into flames, of great walls of fire leaping over roads. Huge trees went up in minutes like sun-dried straw. Cattle caught fire as they charged away from the flames...

1. a. Underline Ⓐ all the structural features you notice in both the paragraph and the individual sentences within it.

   b. What is the impact of this paragraph on the reader? Annotate 🖉 the response with your ideas.

2. Now write 🖉 a paragraph of your own about a fire, deliberately using a list technique to build up power (but choose different details).

.....................................................................................................................................
.....................................................................................................................................
.....................................................................................................................................
.....................................................................................................................................
.....................................................................................................................................
.....................................................................................................................................

## 1 How do I structure paragraphs that engage the reader?

Variation of paragraph and sentence length can be very effective in keeping the reader's interest. Don't be afraid to write occasional incomplete sentences and one-line paragraphs for impact.

**1** **a** Read over what you wrote for Activity 2 on the opposite page. Try adding ✏ a short, alarming sentence about how the fire had quickly become huge and life-threatening – summing up the impact of what you have already written.

.......................................................................................................................

**b** Do you think this sentence would have even more impact as a stand-alone paragraph? Tick ✓.

☐ Yes        ☐ No

**c** Explain ✏ briefly why you think this.

.......................................................................................................................

.......................................................................................................................

It can also be effective to form a paragraph out of an incomplete or minor sentence (a sentence without a verb). For example, after making a statement about the future of an issue, such as 'It would be encouraging if we could look forward to decisive action on this problem from the government', the next paragraph could be, 'Some hope'.

Read the following extract from one student's response to the second task on page 49.

> The soaps slide and slither on and on, taking us into virtual lives that are somehow worse but more entertaining than our own, until many of us need them more than our immediate family, and until our critical faculties are as dull as lead. Do we want to be gradually reduced to intellectual torpor, or do we want to be alert, intelligent, well informed, thoughtful and possessed of taste and critical sense?

**2** **a** Write ✏ a one-sentence paragraph to follow the above. Try using an incomplete sentence.

.......................................................................................................................

**b** Why might this be an effective technique in engaging the reader? Briefly explain ✏ your ideas.

.......................................................................................................................

.......................................................................................................................

Building suspense by withholding a key piece of information until the end of a longer paragraph is another useful tool in the writer's toolkit that helps to keep the reader 'hooked'.

**3** Look back at the paragraph you wrote about the fire. Add ✏ one more sentence, giving important new information about its cause, to leave the reader wanting to find out more.

.......................................................................................................................

.......................................................................................................................

.......................................................................................................................

## 2  How do I experiment with sentence structure to create impact?

Prose has rhythms of its own just as poetry does. If you read sentences aloud, you will begin to hear this, if you are not aware of it already. It is to do with the syntax (the internal arrangement of sentences) and the sounds and lengths of words.

(1) Read these sentences aloud and tick ✓ the one which has more impact.

'To be, or not to be – that is the question.' ☐

'To go on living, or not to, is the problem I'm faced with.' ☐

Can you sense that your preference is partly to do with the rhythm of the words in the sentence?

Read the following two sentences twice, once aloud.

> He felt like the girl in the fairy story – she was told to spin so many yards of cloth by the morning and if she failed she would be the nasty imp's captive forever. However hard he might try, he knew he could not get it done in the time available.

(2) Rewrite ✐ the two sentences, trying to make them sound more fluent.

You may wish to re-order them, shorten them, or split them into shorter sentences for greater impact.

.........................................................................................................................

.........................................................................................................................

.........................................................................................................................

.........................................................................................................................

(3) Now explain ✐ briefly which version flows better and is more effective.

.........................................................................................................................

.........................................................................................................................

> The winds that were blowing in off the desert were becoming the catalyst for a much greater disaster – they blew stronger, and they enraged the flames like bellows, until in the nearby hills firestorms began to erupt.

(4) (a) Rewrite ✐ the sentence above so that it reads with a more pleasing rhythm.

.........................................................................................................................

.........................................................................................................................

.........................................................................................................................

.........................................................................................................................

(b) Read the two versions out loud. Which sounds better and why? ✐

.........................................................................................................................

.........................................................................................................................

.........................................................................................................................

**How do I use advanced punctuation to create impact?**

Some forms of advanced punctuation can help to achieve an overall impression of sophistication in your writing, as long as they are used sparingly. Brackets (and pairs of dashes used as parenthesis in the same way as brackets) can be used for effective 'asides' and emphasis, and ellipsis can be used to create suspense or signal a pause.

Look at the following examples of **parenthesis** from two student responses to the tasks on page 49.

## Paper 1

'Some people' (and here Sanjeev lowered his voice for emphasis) 'say it was arson.'

## Paper 2

Surveys have established – and done so beyond reasonable doubt – that television increases obesity.

(1) What is the effect of the parenthesis in each case? Write ✐ your ideas below.

Paper 1: ....................................................................................................................

Paper 2: ....................................................................................................................

(2) Tick ✓ the effect that you think would be produced if you did this in two consecutive sentences.

It would feel like...

a | ... you were involving the reader more in the narrative. | ☐

b | ...you were trying to hold the reader at arm's length. | ☐

c | ...the punctuation was becoming too obtrusive and blocking the narrative flow. | ☐

d | ...you knew lots of varied punctuation and were using it to good effect. | ☐

An **ellipsis** is commonly used to signal an incomplete sentence, but it is also helpful in narrative when you wish to create a moment of suspense, deliberately withholding – or delaying – some detail, e.g.

But he left, and we knew we would have to wait...

It can be useful in an argument text when you want the reader to think for a second or two before reading on, e.g.

The consequences are all too obvious and worrying...

(4) (a) Write ✐ a sentence of your own which features an ellipsis.

....................................................................................................................

....................................................................................................................

(b) What effect have you achieved here? Explain ✐ your ideas.

....................................................................................................................

....................................................................................................................

# Sample response

To craft paragraphs and sentences that create impact, you need to think about:
- balancing paragraph structure and length
- structuring and ordering sentences to produce a pleasing textual rhythm
- using punctuation carefully and sparingly to add impact to your ideas.

Now look at this exam-style writing task, which you saw earlier in the unit.

'Television is, on the whole, a waste of time.'

Write an article for a broadsheet newspaper explaining your opinion of this statement.   **(40 marks)**

Here is a paragraph from one student's answer:

> Consider the reality TV show for proof that television is a waste of time for the millions who watch these programmes. OK – weird behaviour can be interesting to a lot of people, but why watch this kind of thing? It's like staring at mad people or peering through cracks in the curtains. We shouldn't be doing it. It's prurient. It actually makes us less good people in some strange way. I remember hearing about an episode where for one of their imbecilic recreations it was decided that they should paint a wall using their hands. Some of them decided to do this in swimming costumes and with great enthusiasm one of the men immediately stripped completely and starting daubing paint on the wall with his naked body!

**(1)** How would you improve this paragraph?

**a** Think about how you could alter the structure of the paragraph to engage the reader more readily. Write ✐ some advice for the writer.

.............................................................................................................................

.............................................................................................................................

.............................................................................................................................

**b** Now think about the structure and sequence of ideas in **one or two** sentences. In the box below try restructuring and/or re-ordering ✐ them to produce greater textual rhythm and impact.

**c** Look again at the sentences you have restructured/re-ordered. Could you add impact by adding more advanced punctuation? Write ✐ your thoughts on paper.

# Your turn!

You are now going to write your response to one of these exam-style tasks.

## Paper 1

**Exam-style question**

Write a description suggested by this picture.

(40 marks)

## Paper 2

**Exam-style question**

'Television is, on the whole, a waste of time.'

Write an article for a broadsheet newspaper explaining your opinion of this statement. **(40 marks)**

**(1)** Think about all the different ideas you might include in your response. List ✎ them in the space below.

**(2)** Number ✎ your chosen ideas in the order in which you will use them.

**(3)** Now write ✎ the first two or three paragraphs of your response to your chosen task on paper, thinking carefully about:

- structuring paragraphs that engage the reader
- experimenting with sentence structure to create rhythm and impact
- using advanced punctuation to create impact.

# Review your skills

## Check up

Review your response to the exam-style question on page 55. Tick ✓ the column to show how well you think you have done each of the following.

|  | Not quite ✓ | Nearly there ✓ | Got it! ✓ |
|---|---|---|---|
| structured paragraphs that engage the reader | ☐ | ☐ | ☐ |
| experimented with sentence structure to create impact | ☐ | ☐ | ☐ |
| used advanced punctuation to create impact | ☐ | ☐ | ☐ |

Look over all of your work in this unit. Note down 🖉 three things that you should do to create impact in your paragraphs and sentences.

1. ...........................................................................................................................

2. ...........................................................................................................................

3. ...........................................................................................................................

## Need more practice?

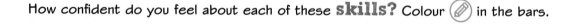

Tackle the other writing task on page 55.

Remember to focus on creating impact and a pleasing rhythm through your choice of paragraph and sentence structure, and through imaginative use of punctuation.

How confident do you feel about each of these **skills?** Colour 🖉 in the bars.

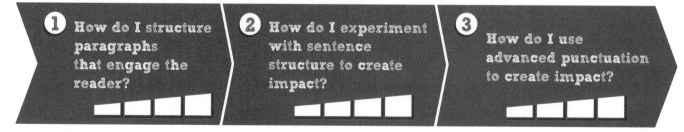

1  How do I structure paragraphs that engage the reader?

2  How do I experiment with sentence structure to create impact?

3  How do I use advanced punctuation to create impact?

# ⑧ Making your meaning clear – choosing precise vocabulary

This unit will help you learn how to select vocabulary to make your meaning as clear as possible. The skills you will build are to:

- choose the right words
- use abstract nouns
- choose the best words.

Good writers command not only a wide vocabulary, but also the skill to use the right word in the right place. Try to be adventurous and use the full range of your vocabulary for maximum clarity, variety and effect.

## Paper 1

**Exam-style question**

Your school or college is asking students to contribute some creative writing for its website.

Write a story about a time when you were fighting against the odds.           **(40 marks)**

## Paper 2

**Exam-style question**

'Despite the obesity epidemic, many of us seem unable to break the habit of eating too much food that is bad for us.'

Write an article for a magazine explaining your views about this statement.           **(40 marks)**

The three key questions in the **skills boosts** will help you to make your meaning clear by choosing precise vocabulary.

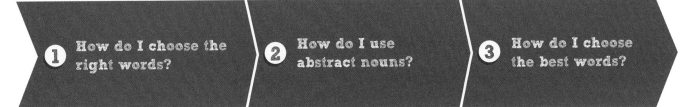

1 How do I choose the right words?

2 How do I use abstract nouns?

3 How do I choose the best words?

Look at the extracts from students' answers to the tasks on page 58.

**Paper 1**

> As I stumbled on, from time to time I almost involuntarily touched Hendrik's letter against my chest, to reassure myself that it was still there. Without the grains of hope that the letter gave me, I might have sunk into the snow at the side of the road and lain there until I lost consciousness. For the border was still two days' journey away, and I did not know if I could make it.
>
> It was bitterly cold, the air damp and icy. I was becoming almost desperate to find somewhere to spend the night, and now the light was fading fast. Soon I could barely see the road. The winds began to howl around me, mingling with wild sounds from the woods.

**Paper 2**

> It is a well-known fact that too many people are obese, and that the figures show that the problem is the worst it has been. Like many other child-related issues in an imperfect world, this has at least something to do with indifferent parenting. Who, after all, decides what the family has for dinner? Who gives out the sweets? In every week, there are many judgements to make for both generations, but who carries the responsibility?
>
> Surveys have shown (as many of us instinctively realise) that 'pester power' all too often resides with choosy children. Weak-willed parents frequently cave in to their demands. One such survey found that a shocking 40 per cent of parents tend to give their heedless offspring exactly what they want.

(1) Look closely at the word choices in the two extracts above.

a Underline (A) any word choices that you think are particularly effective because they seem just right.

b Circle (A) any word choices that you think could be improved, e.g. they might not be precise or interesting enough.

c Annotate (✏) each of the words you have circled, noting:

- **why** you think they should be improved
- **how** you think they could be improved, e.g. give some possible alternative choices.

# 1 How do I choose the right words?

The key elements in writing are the nouns and the verbs – it is these that give the basic structure, momentum and meaning to a sentence. Careful choice of nouns and verbs helps to support your intention and maintain an even and appropriate tone.

Re-read the Paper 1 response below.

> As I stumbled on, from time to time I almost involuntarily touched **Hendrik's letter** against my chest, to reassure myself that it was still there. Without the **grains of hope** that the letter gave me, I might have sunk into the snow at the side of the road and lain there until I lost **consciousness**. For the border was still two days' journey away, and I did not know if I could make it.
>
> It was bitterly cold, the air damp and icy. I was becoming almost desperate to find somewhere to spend the night, and now the light was fading fast. Soon I could barely see the road. The winds began to howl around me, mingling with wild sounds from the woods.

1. Choose one of the nouns or noun phrases in bold and explain how you think the choice of words used has enhanced the extract.

....................................................................................................................................

....................................................................................................................................

....................................................................................................................................

....................................................................................................................................

2. Imagine you are writing a story set on the coast involving a boat. Picture the boat you wish to feature, then think about how much of that image is conveyed by the noun 'boat'.

    a. Write down the most precise noun or noun phrase you can think of to indicate the boat you have in mind. .............................................................................

    b. How many types of tree, flower or bird can you imagine and name? What about cars, houses or food? Try to come up with as many interesting nouns in each category as you can in one minute. Record your ideas on paper.

    Read the response extract above again.

3. a. Underline (A) **all the verbs**.

    b. Now circle (A) the **verbs of motion** again.

    c. How do the verbs of motion help to give a clear picture of what is happening?

    ....................................................................................................................................

    ....................................................................................................................................

4. a. Write down a verb that means 'to walk in a relaxed, unhurried way'. .............................................

    b. Now list as many verbs as you can think of that mean 'walk' in one way or another.

    ....................................................................................................................................

    ....................................................................................................................................

## 2 How do I use abstract nouns?

The nouns explored on the previous page were **concrete** nouns (names of things we can apprehend through at least one of the senses), which help to achieve precision in your writing. To lend authority and sophistication to your writing, however, the accurate use of **abstract** nouns (names of intangible concepts) is a key skill.

1 Tick ✓ the **abstract nouns** in the list below.

| | | | |
|---|---|---|---|
| ☐ diagram | ☐ anger | ☐ government | ☐ hatred |
| ☐ significance | ☐ ambition | ☐ faith | ☐ sample |
| ☐ hope | ☐ joy | ☐ punctuation | ☐ despair |

Powerful narrative and descriptive writing often involves alluding – directly or indirectly – to the emotions. Consider the difference between these pairs of phrases:

| she loathed him | she was consumed with loathing for him | he was so furious | his face flushed with fury |

2 a Underline Ⓐ all the abstract nouns in the lists above that refer to **emotions**.

b Write ✎ a sentence using three of the emotions you have underlined. Try to pack as much power and authority into your sentence as you can.

........................................................................

........................................................................

........................................................................

c Does using an abstract noun instead of an adjective place the narrator closer to the narrative, or further away? Why do you think that is? ✎

........................................................................

3 Now consider the phrase 'lost consciousness' from the Paper 1 answer on page 58.

a Think of an alternative word or phrase with the same meaning. ✎

........................................................................

b Which do you think is more powerful and sophisticated? ✎

........................................................................

c Why do you think the student chose to use an abstract noun in their answer? ✎

........................................................................

Abstract nouns feature strongly in transactional writing. Writers often personify the emotions to lend them extra force, e.g. 'his feelings allowed him no rest', and **personification** is a useful technique to apply. For example 'Prejudice stalks the weak-minded in society and feeds off their fear.'

4 Write ✎ two sentences containing abstract nouns in response to the Paper 2 task on page 57 about obesity. In one of your sentences, try to personify the concept you are discussing, in order to lend extra colour and sophistication to your argument.

........................................................................

........................................................................

# 3 How do I choose the best words?

There are no rules about the best choice of words – so much depends on the context, and perhaps above all on acquiring a good ear for language (just as a musician needs a good ear for music). Understanding when to experiment with ambitious vocabulary and when to favour simplicity is a skill that comes with practice.

Here are some general guidelines with matching activities to help you decide when to risk a more adventurous or elaborate phrase and when to keep things simple.

Avoid **overusing abstract nouns**. If you are not careful, you might produce a sentence such as 'No year passes without evidence of the truth of the statement that government is becoming more complicated'!

**1** Try rewriting ⌀ this sentence in a simpler and clearer form.

..................................................................................................................................................

..................................................................................................................................................

Use **emphatic language**. Fitness adverts don't talk about 'decreasing' fat, but about 'burning' or even 'torching' fat. You don't need to exaggerate in this way in order to achieve the desired effect. A simple but appropriate synonym often carries even more force.

**2** In these examples, replace ⌀ the verb and adverb/adjective in **bold** with a more expressive verb or verb phrase.

**a** The child was in no hurry at all and **walked slowly** [..............................] after his mother.

**b** The teacher was really annoyed now and **shouted loudly** [..............................] at the class.

**c** The argument that television has educational value **seems weak** [..............................] in the face of such low-quality programming.

More ambitious vocabulary can play a useful role in the following contexts:

• detailed description

• expression of feelings

• complex or sophisticated arguments.

**3** In each case, replace ⌀ the word or words in **bold** with a more precise or evocative word or phrase:

**a** A huge **fish** [..............................] had been **washed up** [..............................] on the beach.

**b** The garden pots were **bright** [..............................] with **flowers** [..............................].

**c** I felt **sad** [..............................] and **low** [..............................], and wanted to just **run away and hide** [..............................].

**d** **Judging people** [..............................] on the basis of skin colour should have no **place** [..............................] in our society.

**e** Bullying on social media is **getting worse** [..............................] and is very **upsetting** [..............................] for its victims.

# Sample response

When you select vocabulary for your writing you need to think about:

- choosing the right words
- using abstract nouns where appropriate
- choosing the best words for the context.

**Exam-style question**

'Despite the obesity epidemic, many of us seem unable to break the habit of eating too much food that is bad for us.'

Write an article for a magazine explaining your views about this statement.          **(40 marks)**

Look at these extracts from two student responses to this writing task.

**Student A**

And the producers of yummy foods, such as chocolate, biscuits, chips and crisps, are not exactly unwilling or slow to advertise and package their tempting products with as much colour and humour as they can manage. We don't always understand what they mean exactly...

**Student B**

These days kids are kicking the healthy foods thing: around 80 per cent of parents still give their children white bread instead of the more healthy brown; and no mothers, in a recent survey, said that their children only rarely guzzled chocolates or other sweets. So whose fault is it – kids or their mums?

(1) How effective are these students' vocabulary choices in the two extracts above?

    **a**   Circle (A) any words that do not seem quite right.

    **b**   Underline (A) any phrases where you think abstract nouns might be appropriate.

    **c**   Rewrite (✎) the extracts below, aiming to make the word choices more precise and expressive.

Student A: ...................................................................................................................

........................................................................................................................................

........................................................................................................................................

........................................................................................................................................

........................................................................................................................................

Student B: ...................................................................................................................

........................................................................................................................................

........................................................................................................................................

........................................................................................................................................

........................................................................................................................................

# Your turn!

You are now going to write your response to one of these exam-style tasks.

## Paper 1

**Exam-style question**

Your school or college is asking students to contribute some creative writing for its website.

Write a story about a time when you were fighting against the odds.          **(40 marks)**

## Paper 2

**Exam-style question**

'Despite the obesity epidemic, many of us seem unable to break the habit of eating too much food that is bad for us.'

Write an article for a magazine explaining your views about this statement.          **(40 marks)**

(1) Use the space below to plan your response. Think about all relevant ideas, including any for opening and concluding your answer. Also make a note ✎ of any particularly effective words or phrases that occur to you.

(2) Number ✎ your ideas in the order you intend to use them.

(3) Now write ✎ your response to your chosen task on paper, concentrating on making the right vocabulary choices to help you achieve your intention.

# Review your skills

## Check up

Review your response to the exam-style question on page 63. Tick ✓ the column to show how well you think you have done each of the following.

| | Not quite ✓ | Nearly there ✓ | Got it! ✓ |
|---|---|---|---|
| chosen the right words | ☐ | ☐ | ☐ |
| used abstract nouns | ☐ | ☐ | ☐ |
| chosen the best words | ☐ | ☐ | ☐ |

Look over all of your work in this unit. Note down ✎ three things that you should do to create impact in your paragraphs and sentences.

1. ............................................................................................................

2. ............................................................................................................

3. ............................................................................................................

## Need more practice?

Tackle the other writing task on page 63.

How confident do you feel about each of these **skills?** Colour ✎ in the bars.

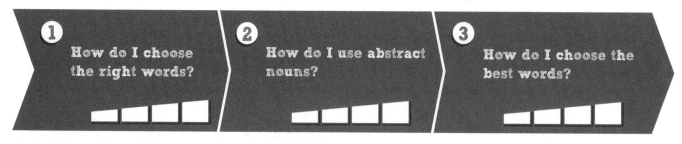

**1** How do I choose the right words?

**2** How do I use abstract nouns?

**3** How do I choose the best words?

# ⑨ Selecting vocabulary for impact and effect

This unit will help you learn how to select vocabulary for impact and effect.
The skills you will build are to:

- explore vocabulary choices and their effects
- use vocabulary choices to enrich your writing
- decide how much figurative language you should use.

In the exam, you will be asked to tackle writing tasks such as the ones below. This unit will prepare you to write your own response to one of these questions.

## Paper 1

**Exam-style question**

Your school or college is asking students to contribute some creative writing for a competition.

Write the opening part of a story about an extremely hot day.    **(40 marks)**

## Paper 2

**Exam-style question**

'Teenagers have to spend too many years at school. No wonder they get bored.'

Write an article for a broadsheet newspaper explaining your point of view on this statement.

   **(40 marks)**

The three key questions in the **skills boosts** will help you to select vocabulary for impact and effect.

**①** How do I explore vocabulary choices and their effects?

**②** How do I use vocabulary choices to enrich my writing?

**③** How much figurative language should I use?

Look at the extracts from students' answers to the tasks above on the next page.

## Paper 1

We were near Basra now, sticky with sweat in the torrid, sweltering desert plain. Through the dusty, fly-strewn windscreen of the jeep, the road appeared as hazy as the horizon, all bleached and burned, dusty and deserted. In the distance, some concrete and steel structures glared at us in the simmering air, and dilapidated trucks and tyres lay strewn about the edges of the road. A dust devil threw a stinging cloud at us, tumbling plastic bottles and whirling bits of paper like strange insects. Suddenly, there emerged out of the heat and dust the vehicles and structures that we instantly recognised as a checkpoint; the hazy outline of the figures declared them to be heavily armed.

## Paper 2

In many tribal communities twelve-year-old boys are treated as men, herding cattle or practising essential crafts. In Kenya you might be hollowing out a mtumbwi (a kind of canoe) from a mango tree. And here in over-educated Britain? Young people are not even allowed their freedom from educational institutions at 16 any more. Many study themselves into a stupor.

It's been said that education is a rather inefficient form of childminding which consists of drumming into children's heads all kinds of knowledge except what will be really useful to them in later life. Do they need to know those French irregular verbs in the past perfect, that chemical formula for plastic? Really we are kidding ourselves – all we do with children is keep them occupied and safe. Most children of 10 have the mental capacity of adults but we make sure they continue to behave like seven-year-olds.

(1) Look closely at the vocabulary choices in the two extracts.

   (a) Underline Ⓐ **four or five** phrases that are effective in answering the exam-style questions.

   (a) Circle Ⓐ the words you think are the most effective within each phrase.

(2) Choose **two** of the phrases you marked as effective. Write ✎ a sentence or two below explaining why you think the vocabulary choices in these phrases are so effective.

......................................................................................................................................

......................................................................................................................................

......................................................................................................................................

......................................................................................................................................

......................................................................................................................................

# 1 How do I explore vocabulary choices and their effects?

One way to make your writing precise and effective is by carefully selecting your vocabulary – choosing between different synonyms can make a significant difference to the impact on the reader.

Look at the phrase below from the student's response to the Paper 1 question on page 66.

> *sticky with sweat in the torrid, sweltering desert plain*

Focus on the word 'sweltering'. Below are some alternatives – synonyms or words with similar connotations.

| baking | ☐ | toasted | ☐ |
| searing | ☐ | | ☐ |
| roasting | ☐ | | ☐ |
| fervid | ☐ | | ☐ |

1. a. Add 🖉 your own ideas for synonyms for 'sweltering' to the list above.

   b. Tick ✓ any words that you think would be effective replacements for 'sweltering'.

   c. Try writing out 🖉 the whole phrase replacing the word 'sweltering' with the option that you think is the most effective.

   .................................................................................................

   d. Which do you prefer? Write 🖉 a sentence explaining your decision.

   .................................................................................................
   .................................................................................................

Read the following clause in which the writer has used some interesting vocabulary.

> *concrete and steel structures <u>glared</u> at us in the <u>simmering</u> air*

2. a. Write 🖉 a sentence explaining why you think the underlined words were chosen. Are they effective?

   .................................................................................................
   .................................................................................................

   b. Now rewrite 🖉 the clause, replacing 'glared' and 'simmering' with synonyms.

   .................................................................................................

   c. Write 🖉 a sentence explaining whether you prefer your version or the original, and why.

   .................................................................................................
   .................................................................................................

# ② How do I use vocabulary choices to enrich my writing?

You know more words than you actually use: so think carefully about the right word to use in the context.

① Read the following sentence.

> In the workshop Alex was busy making repairs to an old car.

Now read these two versions of the same sentence and discuss/think about the differences.

> In the workshop Alex was busy tinkering with the wheels of an old Ford.

> In the noisy workshop Alex was crouched on the concrete replacing the brake discs on an ageing Ford Fiesta.

② **a** In each of the alternative versions, circle Ⓐ the words that add extra detail.

**b** Decide which version you think is best and explain 🖉 why.

........................................................................................................

........................................................................................................

③ **a** Think about concision and economy when writing. Shorten 🖉 the following extract to no more than 15 words, asking yourself what you really need to communicate in a limited space.

> *We were driving, not too fast, in our 2006 jeep along the dual carriageway that runs south through partial desert from Baghdad towards Basra. It was early afternoon, and dust from the rather featureless plain came in irritatingly at the sides of the jeep and blew around our heads.*

........................................................................................................

........................................................................................................

**b** Now rewrite 🖉 your version again, adding several words to improve it in your own way and to create an impact.

........................................................................................................

........................................................................................................

........................................................................................................

**c** How could you further enhance your final version? List 🖉 **four** emotions that the desert drive might cause the writer to feel.

........................................................................................................

........................................................................................................

........................................................................................................

**d** Use one or more of these words to write 🖉 an emotive final sentence that lends the description a more personal impact for the reader.

........................................................................................................

........................................................................................................

## 3 How much figurative language should I use?

Figurative language can show imagination, but may also slow a narrative down. Think about the precise effect you wish to achieve.

**1** Read the following sentence.

> It was as though we were standing in front of a furnace, or a vast dragon had breathed fire all over the land.

**a** Which of the following comments do you agree with? Tick ✐ one or more.

| ☐ These similes work together well. | ☐ The use of two similes creates a 'mixed metaphor' effect, which weakens the effect of each. | ☐ I could probably write a descriptive sentence that was at least as good. |

**b** Have a go at writing ✐ your own simile or metaphor for intense heat or for the sun.

.............................................................................................................................

**2 a** Look at these three sentences. Underline Ⓐ the one you think is most expressive.

> The sun breathed its infinite fire upon us relentlessly and without mercy.

> The sun breathed its relentless fire on us without mercy.

> The sun breathed its fire on us relentlessly and remorselessly.

**b** Write ✐ one brief sentence to explain your choice.

.............................................................................................................................

**c** Now write ✐ your own variation on the same idea.

.............................................................................................................................

Some writers would argue that figurative language gets in the way of the storytelling, and draws too much attention to itself.

**3** Read this opening to a descriptive sentence.

> We cowered from the heat, which dampened our clothes with our own sweat …

Finish ✐ the sentence by adding some further detail. You may wish to use the ideas in the boxes below to help you.

| reddened our faces | irritated our minds | limp bodies |

.............................................................................................................................

.............................................................................................................................

**4** What do you think might be the advantage of using descriptive detail over figurative language? Write ✐ a sentence or two about your views on the merits of each technique.

.............................................................................................................................

.............................................................................................................................

# Sample response

When you select vocabulary for effect, you should think about:

- using some of the less common words you know
- using figurative language for greater impact.

**1** Read this extract from one student's response to the Paper 2 exam-style writing task.

> In many tribal communities twelve-year-old boys are treated as men, herding cattle or practising essential crafts. In Kenya you might be hollowing out a mtumbwi (a kind of canoe) from a mango tree. And here in over-educated Britain? Young people are not even allowed their freedom from educational institutions at 16 any more. Many study themselves into a stupor.
>
> It's been said that education is a rather inefficient form of childminding which consists of drumming into children's heads all kinds of knowledge except what will be really useful to them in later life. Do they need to know those French irregular verbs in the past perfect, that chemical formula for plastic? Really we are kidding ourselves – all we do with children is keep them occupied and safe. Most children of 10 have the mental capacity of adults but we make sure they continue to behave like seven-year-olds.

**a** What is the writer's intention in the first paragraph? Write ✐ a sentence or two explaining your ideas.

.................................................................................................

.................................................................................................

.................................................................................................

**b** What is their intention in the second? Write ✐ a sentence or two explaining your ideas.

.................................................................................................

.................................................................................................

.................................................................................................

**c** Choose two interesting words or phrases from the extract. Explain ✐ in each case why it is interesting or effective.

.................................................................................................

.................................................................................................

.................................................................................................

.................................................................................................

.................................................................................................

**d** Choose two words or phrases to which you think you could supply an engaging alternative. Write down ✐ the word or phrase from the response with your own alternative alongside.

...................................................        ...................................................

...................................................        ...................................................

# Your turn!

You are now going to write your response to one of these exam-style tasks.

**Paper 1**

**Exam-style question**

Your school or college is asking students to contribute some creative writing for a competition.

Write the opening part of a story about an extremely hot day. **(40 marks)**

**Paper 2**

**Exam-style question**

'Teenagers have to spend too many years at school. No wonder they get bored.'

Write an article for a broadsheet newspaper explaining your point of view on this statement.

**(40 marks)**

(1) Think about all the different ideas you might include in your response. Note them in the space below as you plan your answer. Add all relevant ideas, including any for opening and ending your response, and any effective phrases that occur to you.

(2) Number your ideas in the order in which you will use them.

(3) Now write your response to your chosen task on paper, focusing on making the right vocabulary choices to help you achieve your aims.

# Review your skills

## Check up

Review your response to the exam-style question on page 71. Tick ⟨✓⟩ the column to show how well you think you have done each of the following.

|  | Not quite ⟨✓⟩ | Nearly there ⟨✓⟩ | Got it! ⟨✓⟩ |
|---|---|---|---|
| explored vocabulary choices and their effects | ☐ | ☐ | ☐ |
| used vocabulary choices to enrich my writing | ☐ | ☐ | ☐ |
| decided how much figurative language to use | ☐ | ☐ | ☐ |

Look over all your work in this unit. Note down ⟨✎⟩ three things that you should remember to do when choosing vocabulary and three things that you should remember not to do when choosing vocabulary.

DO:

1. ......................................................................................................

2. ......................................................................................................

3. ......................................................................................................

DON'T:

1. ......................................................................................................

2. ......................................................................................................

3. ......................................................................................................

## Need more practice?

Tackle the other writing task on page 71. Time yourself and try to complete it in about 45 minutes.

Remember to focus closely on selecting, reviewing and improving vocabulary choices to help you to achieve your intention.

How confident do you feel about each of these **skills?** Colour ⟨✎⟩ in the bars.

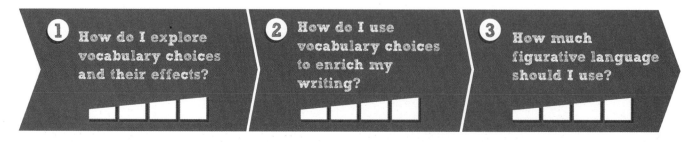

**1** How do I explore vocabulary choices and their effects?

**2** How do I use vocabulary choices to enrich my writing?

**3** How much figurative language should I use?

# Answers

## Unit 1

### Page 2

① Inviting us to identify with the first-person narrator; dealing with strong feelings; leading to a violent climax.

② For example, involving the narrator with another character, maybe of the opposite sex.

### Page 3

① 1B, 2C, 3D, 4E, 5F, 6A

② For example, if you wanted to bring out a moral message, the plan might include some discussion of people's rights, and a pointed conclusion.

### Page 4

① Draw the reader in to a static or dynamic scene or situation.

③ For example, a chronological outline might look like this:

| The beach at dawn in summer. | People walking dogs, etc. around 9 am. | A crowd quickly gathers and occupies it after 10 am. | Focus on various little groups throughout the day. |
|---|---|---|---|

④ For example, a 'camera angles' outline might look like this:

| Aerial view of the beach. | Panoramic view of whole beach; perhaps 'panning' along the beach from one side to the other. | Zooming in on various groups or individuals. | Zooming out to the 'long shot' panorama again, or aerial view. |
|---|---|---|---|

## Unit 2

### Page 10

① Many famous people are wonderful role models, but the modern celebrity often is not.

④ Examples could be scientists, artists, musicians both from the past, e.g. Alexander Fleming, Van Gogh, Beethoven, and the present, e.g. Stephen Hawking, Anish Kapoor, David Bowie.

### Page 12

② For example:

I do not feel remotely taken in by the ridiculous hype surrounding modern celebrities…

I witnessed the adverse effects of imitating the celebrity lifestyle in the case of a friend of mine two years ago…

Eating disorders are now a serious problem among young women who have been negatively influenced by media portrayals of celebrity diets, fashion choices…

### Page 14

② For example: One of the advantages in looking at figures from the past is that we can study their whole lives – how, for example, they might have worked immensely hard to achieve what they did; or how they might have done great things for love.

## Unit 3

### Page 19

② See the story structure table on page 22 as an example.

### Page 20

① *How it engages our interest:* for example, **A** arouses our curiosity about the 'monsters' by hinting at their dangers without giving anything away; also provides a touch of suspense by mentioning the ominous weather and using the intriguing phrase 'pathetic fallacy'.

② For example: **B** – 'my blurred world': because it suggests very economically that her world is both speeding past and is also blurred mentally or emotionally – also hints that the character might be in tears.

### Page 21

① For example:

A *Advantages:* could be very engaging to younger readers; could be used for teenage humour. *Disadvantages:* restricts the way the story is presented to the reader, if there is no other narrative voice.

## Unit 4

### Page 26

② For example, make the 4th point the introduction, and the 3rd the conclusion.

③ For example, the effect of the rhetorical question might be to make the conclusion more forceful.

④ *Other points:* For example: The Labour government was implementing a huge scheme to modernise Britain's schools, but it stopped less than half-way through: why can we not continue it?

*Other techniques:* See page 28 for examples.

### Page 28

② For example:

*alliteration:* We must act now to safeguard standards and put faith in the future;
*hyperbole:* The absolute minimum our children deserve is this…

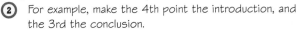

**(3)** An anecdote might begin like one of the examples given, then develop with a few details, e.g. Morrissey has said that he had a great music teacher who let him and his friends play for hours in the band-room, and he even helped out sometimes on the keyboards…

## Page 29

**(1)** For example, points 5 and 6 about DT and music could be merged.

**(3)** *Some people who dropped out of school might think that…many teenagers feel bored and unfulfilled at school and would rather be in the real world learning skills and earning money.*

## Page 30

**(1)** For example, points 1 and 2 could be reversed for greater impact (argument followed by counter-argument). The plan needs to supply more detail and evidence overall – see the plans on pages 26 and 28 for further ideas.

# Unit 5

## Page 34

**(1)** **Paper 1:** For example, the quite long, complex sentences that make up a good deal of this response help to achieve fluency and rhythm; the numbers of adjectives, sometimes in pairs (e.g. 'cloudless sunny skies'), help to make it flow because adjectives carry less of the 'weight' in sentences than do nouns and verbs.

**Paper 2:** For example, the colloquial language helps give it a conversational fluency and a lively, spontaneous impact.

**(2)** For example, in the Paper 2 answer, the way that the last sentence switches from a statement to a question means that the structure could be stronger.

## Page 35

**(1)** For example: first, second, then, next, meanwhile, later, eventually, finally.

**(2)** For example: as a result, moreover, yet.

## Page 36

**(1)** This passage moves the reader on by picking up an element of the scene from the end of one paragraph ('great chimneys', 'solid blocks') and **referring back** to it at the start of the next using a pronoun ('They') and a synonym ('these monoliths').

**(2)** For example: trains/train, he/him, awakening/awake

**(3)** For example: 'In Thomas's flat, gradually the noise from outside began to make itself felt…'

## Page 37

**(1)** For example: well-known/popular; press/gossip columns/chat shows; encourage/motivate; adore/have a crush on; damaging/negative.

**(2)** For example: The first sentence introduces a counter-argument by saying that there are some who don't agree with the argument of the first paragraph.

## Page 38

**(1)** **a** For example: 'it was when I had to look after my grandfather quite a lot of the time because I was living in his house doing my GCSEs (because we have moved house but I didn't want to change schools)'

**b** For example: 'It was after my family had moved house, but I had gone to live with my grandfather so I didn't have to change schools during my GCSEs: I had to spend quite a lot of time looking after him.'

# Unit 6

## Page 42

**(1)** There is no correct answer: perhaps the first is more clearly and fluently written because it is focused on a series of details we can imagine clearly, whereas the second is slightly vague or loose in parts (e.g. 'a landscape with many different routes through it') and overall gives a more gratuitously 'wordy' impression.

**(2)** **a** **Feature 1:** variety and sophistication of vocabulary.

**Feature 2:** use of pathetic fallacy (misery and bitter wind).

**b** **Feature 1:** emphatic short sentences.

**Feature 2:** use of analytical phrases such as 'academic, social, economic'.

## Page 43

**(1)** **a** It is short, emotive and emphatic, summing up his feelings.

**b** For example: 'bombarded' is a powerful and dynamic verb; 'waves' intensifies the feeling of vulnerability.

**c** Another very short sentence which strikes a positive note simply and emphatically.

**d** The imperative addresses the reader and urges them to engage with the argument.

**(2)** For example: 'We're trying to forget the revision we need to do to get a decent job.'

**(3)** Use some of the sentences in this unit as possible models.

## Page 44

**(1)** For example: 'We often begin sentences in conversations with "and" or "but", so to do so in writing makes the style seem conversational and spontaneous: this can help engage the reader in something that feels like a dialogue.'

**(2)** For example: 'It involves the reader, inviting them to join with the writer and others in some action or way of thinking that will make a difference.'

# Unit 7

## Page 50

**(1)** **a** For example: short and straightforward first sentence, with the key word 'started'; longer, more complex second sentence, using three present participles for unity and pattern, emphasising progression; simple past tense forms 'accelerated', 'caught', 'charged' make information more frightening as paragraph continues.

    **b**  For example: 'It draws the reader into a scene of horrific destruction by building up and intensifying the description as it goes on.'

## Page 51

**2**  **a**  '(I'll go for) the latter.'

    **b**  Adopting a question and answer method is effective in engaging the reader in a discussion.

## Page 52

**2**  For example: 'He felt like the girl in the fairy story who had to spin so many yards of cloth by the morning, otherwise she would be the nasty little imp's captive forever. But he knew he could not get it done.'

**4**  See the version on page 50.

## Page 53

**1**  **Paper 1**: By delaying what the character says, and telling us that he lowered his voice, implying that the information is secret, the parenthesis both creates suspense and places more emphasis on the key word at the end ('arson').

    **Paper 2**: The effect here is to give the assertion at the end of the sentence more weight and authority.

**2**  c

## Page 54

**1**  **a**  For example, the first sentence could be restructured to make its point more effectively; the second feels rather 'loose' and a bit too chatty; the next four sentences involve some repetition and could be edited; the painting example might be made more forceful if it were followed by a short concluding sentence, rather than ending the paragraph as it does.

    **b**  For example, the first sentence could be rewritten: 'For evidence that television is surely a waste of time on a large scale, consider the reality TV show.'

# Unit 8

## Page 58

**1**  **b**  For example, in extract 2: 'the worst it has been'; 'indifferent'; 'a shocking'.

## Page 59

**1**  'Hendrik's letter' provides a 'prop' for the character; in other words it gives us an object on which clearly hangs a tale – in addition, it is associated with another character, which increases our interest; 'grains of hope' is a metaphor that has the effect of making hope seem concrete, measurable and very scarce; 'consciousness' has a link with 'life' – so it suggests he might lose it altogether.

**2**  **a**  For example: 'stroll'; 'amble'; 'saunter'; 'dawdle'; 'meander'; 'wander'.

## Page 60

**1**  **a**  All except 'diagram', 'punctuation' and 'sample'.

**2**  **a**  'hope', 'anger', 'joy', 'hatred', 'despair'.

    **c**  It tends to distance the narrator slightly from the character because he is focusing on what the impersonal emotion is doing, rather than on the person feeling the emotion.

**3**  **a**  'fell asleep'.

    **b**  For example: 'Lost consciousness' is more powerful than 'fell asleep' partly because the word 'lost' makes it sound more negative, and partly because the phrase carries a suggestion that he might never wake up.

## Page 61

**1**  For example: 'Every year brings evidence of the growing complexity of government.'

**2**  **a**  'dawdled'    **b**  'bellowed'    **c**  'collapses'.

**3**  Consult a thesaurus if stuck!

# Unit 9

## Page 66

**2**  For example: 'A dust devil threw a stinging cloud at us': firstly, there is precision in the use of the term 'dust devil', which helps us to visualise it; next, the strong verb 'threw' adds a dynamic touch, and finally the adjective 'stinging' is vivid and brings in another sense (touch/pain).

## Page 68

**2**  **b**  The third sentence is arguably the best because it is the most precise and helps us to imagine the scene in the greatest detail.

**3**  **a**  For example, 'The dust of the afternoon desert blew in our faces as we steadily approached Basra.'

## Page 69

**1**  **a**  The use of two similes creates a 'mixed metaphor' effect, which weakens the effect of each.

**4**  Figurative language tends to add impact, imaginative energy, and liveliness, sometimes humour; descriptive detail adds precision, and sensory effects – it is often more appropriate when the writer is trying to make the reader 'see' the scene.

## Page 70

**1**  **a**  For example: 'The writer is trying to show by stark contrast how little freedom of choice teenagers have in this country.'

    **b**  For example: 'Here the writer is intending, by exaggerating his points, to make the reader see that children are pointlessly over-educated.'

    **c**  For example: 'The word 'drumming' is an effective metaphorical verb since it makes the method of education appear bullying and repetitive, without imagination or thought.'

    **e**  Words or phrases you might pick include 'in later life', 'rather', 'really' and 'kidding ourselves'.

Published by Pearson Education Limited, 80 Strand, London, WC2R ORL.

www.pearsonschoolsandfecolleges.co.uk

Text © Pearson Education Limited 2017
Produced and typeset by Tech-Set Ltd, Gateshead
Original illustrations © Pearson Education Ltd 2017

The right of Robert O'Brien to be identified as author of this work has been asserted by him in accordance with the Copyright, Designs and Patents Act 1988.

First published 2017

20 19 18
10 9 8 7 6 5 4 3

**British Library Cataloguing in Publication Data**
A catalogue record for this book is available from the British Library

ISBN 978 0435 18324 0

Printed in Italy by Lego S.p.A

**Acknowledgements**
The publisher would like to thank the following for their kind permission to reproduce their photographs:

(Key: b-bottom; c-centre; l-left; r-right; t-top)

**Alamy Images:** Alex Segre 1, LOOK Die Bildagentur der Fotografen GmbH 17, 23, 24; **Rex Shutterstock:** London News Pictures 8; **U.S. Department of Agriculture (USDA):** 49, 50, 55

All other images © Pearson Education

This workbook has been developed using the Pearson Progression Map and Scale for English.

To find out more about the Progression Scale for English and to see how it relates to indicative GCSE 9–1 grades go to www.pearsonschools.co.uk/ProgressionServices

### Helping you to formulate grade predictions, apply interventions and track progress.

Any reference to indicative grades in the Pearson Target Workbooks and Pearson Progression Services is not to be used as an accurate indicator of how a student will be awarded a grade for their GCSE exams.

You have told us that mapping the Steps from the Pearson Progression Maps to indicative grades will make it simpler for you to accumulate the evidence to formulate your own grade predictions, apply any interventions and track student progress. We're really excited about this work and its potential for helping teachers and students. It is, however, important to understand that this mapping is for guidance only to support teachers' own predictions of progress and is not an accurate predictor of grades.

Our Pearson Progression Scale is criterion referenced. If a student can perform a task or demonstrate a skill, we say they are working at a certain Step according to the criteria. Teachers can mark assessments and issue results with reference to these criteria which do not depend on the wider cohort in any given year. For GCSE exams however, all Awarding Organisations set the grade boundaries with reference to the strength of the cohort in any given year. For more information about how this works please visit: https://www.gov.uk/government/news/setting-standards-for-new-gcses-in-2017